Ken

ARRIVE D... AT THE SAME PLACE

AUSTIN MACAULEY PUBLISHERS™
LONDON * CAMBRIDGE * NEW YORK * SHARJAH

Copyright © Ken Eaton-Dykes 2024

The right of Ken Eaton-Dykes to be identified as the author of this work has been asserted by the author in accordance with sections 77 and 78 of the Copyright, Designs and Patents Act 1988.

All rights reserved. No part of this publication may be reproduced, stored in a retrieval system, or transmitted in any form or by any means, electronic, mechanical, photocopying, recording, or otherwise, without the prior permission of the publishers.

Any person who commits any unauthorised act in relation to this publication may be liable to criminal prosecution and civil claims for damages.

A CIP catalogue record for this title is available from the British Library.

ISBN 9781035829798 (Paperback)
ISBN 9781035829804 (ePub e-book)

www.austinmacauley.com

First Published 2024
Austin Macauley Publishers Ltd®
1 Canada Square
Canary Wharf
London
E14 5AA

1

This poem is a sentimental little verse about two little girls who happen to be my great-grandchildren. Have you noticed the older one gets, besides learning about the basic aspects of life, you find during that passage of time, each aspect is ever more a pixellated mass of implication to be interpreted as best you can and passed on for the well-being of your less experienced successors?

GREAT-GRANDKIDS

Each grinning sits astride my old rheumatic knees
a pair of exuberant saplings
aged just four rings and three
two new babies born in the woods
impatiently broke from swelling buds
off a sturdy family tree

roots mulched firm bedded deep
fed by antecedents in their everlasting sleep
flourishing, fixed, to a healthy mix
of assorted ancestry.

Untiring, unbridled, undaunted, unfearing,
Wide-eyed, so cute, delightful, endearing
escaped to the sky from the dappled dark clearing
dazzling arrays of new things to be gleaning.
Halting enquiries launch life's learning curve
curiosity heightens, hard-wired verve.

"Why was Jack Horner sat in a corner
with an enormous pie?"
"why was Mary quite contrary?"
eyes demand an instant reply
He was looking for somewhere to put his thumb
maybe find and eat a delicious plum
I return with a wearisome sigh.

From small beginnings, we learn to fly
some find it a struggle
but succeed by and by
Shy, meek, outgoing, mild,
geeky, reserved, or outrageously wild
Be patient, be gentle, think love is all.

There's no growing wrong
only upward and strong
from pools of sweet memory
imbibed on recall.

Just when your children's children have blossomed into "what you hope" are successful responsible adults, is it a time to take stock of your relationships worth? and together strengthened with the benefit of hindsight, look back on and agree it was time well spent. But now has evolved into a quiet, slightly boring, unproductive, not much going on, fallow period between generation building.

Then what do you know along in rapid succession a third crop of great-grandchildren arrive for us their great-grandparents to again search out and dust the many books of nursery rhymes and fairy tales we had sung and recited to their excited, and equally eager-to-learn predecessors.

Plus the oft' repeated instance when three-year-olds finish crawling on your knee, sit motionless concentrating wide-eyed, unblinking, intently contemplating your once young hairy nostrils.

Then suddenly perking up, they dismiss the image to the backs of their curiosity-sated minds, for retrieval as a vague recollection, during future moments of déjà vu.

Rocket science has been around longer than you might think. Starting in New Testament times albeit in a primitive way at the holiest period of the Christian calendar.

It was Ingenious mathematical timing guaranteed that Jesus didn't ascend prematurely like a rocket on a stick, that Friday.

It was two thousand years later a plausible explanation for the ascension emerged when pensioners Tom and Tess decided to end it all in a way that was not as original as they thought.

TOM AND TESS'S BUDGET FLIGHT

Sat sitting in their quaint old-fashioned
forties style front room
a ninety-year-old couple
contemplate impending doom.

We've dwelt contented in this house
for sixty years and more
most of them were happy
excepting three or four.

Gazing at the blazing fire
each smilingly recalls
frozen moments in old pictures
hung around familiar walls.

I've been thinking, said old Tom out loud
to his adoring spouse,
it's getting to the time
we can't maintain our little house.

I don't want to be a burden
and neither I think do you
so I've made a plan
for an easy way out
simultaneously for two.

You mean to enact a suicide pact
she responded with mounting concern.
There's a growing trend towards multiple ends
for them lonely… with nowhere to turn.

But what about God's holy teachings
regarding… do it yourself demise
they say he gets very angry
not invited, to supervise.

You don't have to worry my darling
we'll accomplish the whole thing with ease
on larger than average helpings
of cabbage and marrowfat peas.

Neighbours worried, enquire to each
have you seen old Tom and Tess
Constable breaks door down
the quicker to access.
Staggers back in horror
at the smell and rasping sounds
from a pair of bloated corpses
levitating off the ground.

After the embalming
the mortician and his missis
completed the job on Tom and Tess
plugging up… their orifices.

friends in pews at the Crematorium
unaware of swelling methane
in Tess and Tom's dead tums
were suddenly sent reeling.
When both as one, burst coffin lids
and shot up to the ceiling.
Straight through a stained glass fanlight
like rockets towards Heaven
scared the shit from all aboard
a passing seven four seven.
Down at the Crematorium
the Vicar's looking pleased
even though it looks as though
he'll not get any fees.

For Tom and Tess leave scorch marks
hurtling through the trees.
He sits broadly smiling,
in the artificial breeze.

Now certain of what Tucker
was served at the last supper,
from which Jesus heartily ate,
and shared with his Disciples
off a larger-than-average plate.

Gets in touch with his local Bishop
on his mobile phone by text
breathlessly, sends a thesis
of what likely happened next.

While Peter and Paul,
proposed a world tour
eating soup of the day and cheese.
Jesus planning an exit
that would bring them to their knees
scoffed a bigger-than-average helping
of cabbage and marrowfat peas.

So if you want to spike convention
and care to emulate
choose the luxury, or alternate
cheap affordable rate.

Number One's the best of produce
organic, and sure to please.
Or the TESCO everyday blast off
supercharged with their own mushy peas.

The committee on global warming I hear
are now overwhelmingly keen,
to subsidise funeral expenses
on condition, we all go green.

Burial grounds redundant
the future resting place,
is spinning around the Milky Way,
on the outer edge of space.
Buy yourself a telescope
and on Sunday afternoon
catch a glimpse of Gran and Grandpa
orbiting the moon.

There's a small blue plaque
on that quaint little house
dedicated to Tom, and his loving old spouse,
I mustn't forget to mention.
Donated by Richard Dawkins
For busting the myth of ascension.

RHYMING TIMES

I'd like the below piece on the inside of the back cover.

I've travelled countless millions of miles during my life on this vehicle we call Earth, without getting anywhere beyond where I am now. This repetitive circling seems to be the fundamental principle necessary for the upkeep of boring annuals like Christmas, Wimbledon, and Bake Off.

Oh how much more interesting my life could have been? might Earth have taken a straight trajectory now and again. For a welcome departure to the usual spin of things.

I'm just like any other old person wondering where all the time went sat here slowing down, recapitulating events till the finishing post came into view.

AT LAST, I KNOW NOW WHERE I'M @

Thinking of things as you do
why am I me why are you, you
frogs, insects, them in the zoo
what are we all put down here to do?

Conceived from cuddles and kisses
That's wonderful, that's fine,
it's unfortunate from the outset though
We're in permanent decline.

Been on this earth a long time now
eighty years, and plenty
soon I'll be moving I don't know where.
My bed, left cold, and empty
I've written many theories
as to why, and what life's for,
gave up, without an answer
don't care much anymore.

Quite spritely for my age, it's said
often out to dine
An avid listener of Radio Four
Brew beer, and ferment wine
have had a go at making jam
Strawberry, raspberry, plum
can climb up steps to decorate
still able to wipe my bum.

I'm way off the elusive answer
for a reason to exist
have lost my curiosity now
for what humanity persists.
After stoic competition
in the uphill human race
The explanation as to,

"what's it about"
has been staring me in the face.

Mental pictures of my future
were obscured by irrational fears
when the job interviewer asked me
where I'd be in fifty years.
Disciplined since different regimes
time measured by ticking clocks
today if asked the same question
I'd with certainty say in a box
thumbing through those bygone days
signposted
ups and downs,
the periods of happiness
outnumber many frowns.

While fellow peers, forge second careers
I live in a sheltered flat,
eat a healthy diet
pass time doing this and that
I'm certainly not wealthy,
and there're things I can't afford,
but I've stumbled across the meaning of life
like him who found the lost chord.

My reward for that eighty-year struggle
over life's symbolic miles
is two gorgeous great granddaughter's.
Heart melting innocent smiles.

2

This is how I imagine someone, after following a life of shadowy deference, say for instance a faithful old servant would prepare for the minimum inconvenience to his master. Post the casting of his mortal coil.

THE END TO A PERFECT WAY

I've tried to please,
put others at ease
went out of my way to be friendly
clean smart warm of heart
innovative, regarded as trendy.
Heard New Year's Day chimes eighty-eight times
been subject to four different Monarchs
heard George the Fifth, do the first Christmas speech
and MP's disingenuous bollocks.

Unaccomplished, pleasant of mind
academically non-inclined
a pragmatic logical thinker.
Able, efficient, do things without fuss
So "IF" life's an exam… I'll get a B plus

Each night I bathe, drink a large glass of wine
don a white dressing gown purchased online
the best of material, trimmed with black
from the finest tailor bespoken.

Climb onto the bed, bones protest with a crack
hands crossed on my chest, lying still on my back
a position I've trained to hold steady.
Then if I'm taken, during the night.
They'll find me laid out. Oven ready.

And so is put to rest yet another introvert serf, modelled by DNA and inclined (gene-wise) to be a hand rag for his betters.

A bad enough end you might think, but really not such a poor fate when compared to the infinite variety of imperfect genetically permutations with which significant numbers of our present society are unfortunately infected, leading them eventually into displaying unspeakable evils of varying intensity, by way of natural tendencies inherited from an ancestry rich in psychotic antecedents.

What's an antecedent, sir? "Jones" If you only knew of the many occasions you have Soooooh nearly been one.

It's hard enough to find a job these days, but even worse if you're born with a very sensitive laughing gene, that could almost be described as a disability. Alright at parties, but embarrassing around Granddad's death bed. having a good sense of humour is okay in its place, but first, you need to know which situations are appropriate.

SMILES

I'm a unique inhabitant of this earth
with predisposed uncontrollable mirth
when placed in the cot
number four in the litter
an astonished Nurse exclaimed
could've sworn, I heard a titter.

Mother lying on the bed
throbbing hips aching head
grimacing at stretch marks
over sore lactating tit, says
I'm really glad, SOME buggers
seen the funny side of it.

Growing up in this large brood
and always in a happy mood
got more slaps than the other three
for laughing when I shouldn't be
social services got involved
making a twenty-four hour graph
of me smiling, chuckling, giggling,
between side-splitting belly laughs
the occupational therapist looked thoughtfully and then said
I find this case most puzzling, he's difficult to assess
having never seen a case like this
I reservedly acquiesce,
to your having a few more quid a week,
apply to the DSS.

Having never heard of an illness as such
a condition brought on by laughing too much
officials conferring took hours to agree
that until the time we can or will,
discover a cure, maybe a pill,
to make your son more miserable,
we're willing to go those extra miles
and award him benefits, for involuntary smiles.

Meanwhile,
find him a job,
hard manual action,
where laughing won't be
too big a distraction.

Despairing of finding a job location
I stumbled upon my true vocation
laughing at comedians, in a home
suffering severe "unfunny syndrome."

I was paid to grin and giggle
at unbelievably bad jokes
split my sides at conundrums
till I was fit to choke,
peals of laughter, permanent chuckles,
nonstop crudities near the knuckle
nighttime rich with double entendres
tales of French knickers, ladies' suspenders
learner drivers, the highway code
and why the chicken crossed the road.

Now retired, on my own
memories return of that rehab home
I count amongst my circle of friends
hundreds of unfunny comedians.

Now! What of that famous leghorn
performing its road-crossing tricks?
Just a built-in genetical mission
"he was after pulling chicks."

Being realistic as we no doubt should
he ended up like most chickens would
Kentucky deep fried, finger-lickin' good,
deep down suppose, I don't really care
the times he crossed that thoroughfare

I fall about, laughing still
the reasons are uncountable.
I hear the last time he crossed the road
was to see a hardcore movie
when the lights went down he gave a frown
got very upset and deluded
instead of the advertised,
Flock Around The Cock,
it was Batteries Not Included.

REFLECTIONS ON MANS FINAL JOURNEY

Celibate Priests, Fundamentalist Imams,
eagerly preach their delusive plans
Protestant Vicars and Methodist lay,
give it out in gentler ways,
to simple folk in hallowed halls
with pointy tops, round minarets,
brass artefacts, smooth marble steps.

The use of loud hailers and noisy bells
call the faithful to worship and god to please
devotions observed on bended knees,
while venerable leaders in a vigorous dispute
offer paths to Heaven by differing route
on varying surfaces stony or smooth,
stony seems the most "with it" groove.

Walk up, walk up, walk up this way,
walk up for sentence on judgement day,
when your average decent Joe and Jane
hoping years of piety were not in vain,
smile as they anticipate
the joy, the peace, tranquillity,
beyond that pearly gate.

The suicide bomber with the quickening pace
savours pleasures awaiting, Heaven within,
can't wait to ravage, his first virgin,
anxious, impatient, full of self-important worth.
Hope she's not so ugly
as his last act on Earth.

Now the time has come to be profound
'cause when we're dead and in the ground,
having lost all emotion and concupiscence
perform the same task in unison,
decaying slowly without strife,
compulsory cohesion,
preposterous in life.

3

REMEMBERING THE HOLOCAUST

Honouring Holocaust victims
on the evening of last Monday week
reliving unspeakable horrors
through articulate rhyme and speech
we were made aware and reminded
listening silently in a mournful array
those despicable thoughts
fired by hate long ago
lurk latent in hearts still today.

Awakened from restive slumber
"New Order" perverted beliefs
will repeat old agendas, long-term aims
virulent hatred fills vacuum brains
reviving the dream, inflicting the pain
death on the street,
cruel fair-haired elite.

Fervent disciples sow tainted seed
threshed from rich harvests of dogmatised creed
engineered with the aforethought intention
to inflame once benign, now possessed open minds
into acts, of inhuman aggression.

Smother the blazing incitements
igniting impassioned breasts.
Extinguish the source of misleading news
divisive rhetoric, perverted views
these blinkered malefactors profess.
For only sincere, altruistic love
will Malevolence.
Forever, suppress.

The long cycle of the 1930s generation is rapidly bringing to completion its temporary task of being trusted with the overall welfare of the planet and that of its population. But instead of using this precious time united as one voice to achieve social cohesion through fair trade, it is still being used as in the previous two centuries, insidiously by unscrupulous political leaders and businessmen for the deliberate exploitation of politically naive, leaders in underdeveloped countries to their nefarious advantage with, "in the beginning" enticement with bags of salt, followed by a mixture of veiled threats, and two-faced diplomacy. Backed up by the silhouette of a gunboat on the horizon.

Hatred towards the atrocity-led policies from the past three centuries, continues to echo from out the still open sores of yester-year conflicts.

Instead of uniting together. Prospering nations competing for trade ultimately chose to face each other in a violent confrontation. when broken treaties and ignored threats ripened into war, and not the handshaking sincere honest cooperation needed to build an internationally controlled peaceful future for a world where all of humanity would be equal in every respect, and minorities not graded for special treatment.

THE INSIDIOUS PROCESS OF DECAY

From being young, having seen, been told
I've had this fear of growing old
a joint creaking, pill-taking, medicinal hell
encompassed in an atmospheric,
geriatric smell.

But now I've gotten old myself
no hair, few teeth fell off the shelf
in reasonable health though poor in wealth
I'm not depressed ill or sad
this being old "is not so bad"
I'm feeling fit and keeping well
recite bad poems at the Ring O'Bell
no inhibitions confident bolder
don't suffer (I think) old people's odour.

The best of my day has got to be
after dark when it's time for tea
smug warm wanting for nowt
pile food on the plate, proceed to pig out

a large glass of wine then two then many
find the remote, switch on the telly.

Antiques Roadshow, Clarkson top gears
Ant and Dec, The Three Musketeers
dash from the bathroom after a pee
don't want to miss what's next on TV
but the drink kicks in it's not to be
collapse flat outstretched on the settee.

Three in the morning wake and rally
missed the end of Downton Abbey
stomach rumbles need food to ingest
snack on dried gravy peeled off my chest
discard the underpants socks and vest
lay weary head on the flat pillow to rest.

Vibrating snores ripple stubbled cheek
good job I drink only twice a week
content as a babe asleep in its cot
one happy wine-stained old bundle of grott.
The whole place needs cleaning
losing the plot
couldn't care less, if I'm smelly or not.

4

Sunday 3rd September is the anniversary of the beginning of WW2, which left "eighty-five" million people dead. This piece contains personal memories of that time, plus a few thoughts on events up to the present. Where we all take for granted and do not appreciate the much higher standards of living enjoyed today. The hard lessons learned from the past are long forgotten and the European Community born out of that conflict is threatened with a return to the dis-unity of those times that helped spawn the tragedies of World Wars I and II.

There will never be peace in the world. But we can at least "TRY" to minimise the likelihood of war, by patiently, from small beginnings, working towards global unification.

WE REMEMBER THE KILLING. BUT FORGET THE FUTILITY OF IT

War's over and finished, an age since it started.
Was a nine-year-old nipper when Chamberlain imparted
that World War II, he'd reluctantly started
"We won't let our friends the Polish people down"
he declared through a worried, of the consequence's frown.

Church bells were stilled into silence, that warm September day
till the end of that obscene, six-year bloody affray.

It's May forty-five, I'm a grubby adolescent
much bigger than Mum, obnoxious, unpleasant
not the same person when Father had gone
battling the Germans in 1941.
Mum was worried, felt sorry for her
but perked up when she saw
as I ate my breakfast toast
the blue-edged airmail letter among the morning post
later after school sitting down to tea
reopening the envelope she read out loud to me
what I thought were exciting fun, the things our dad had seen and done,
driving a lorry, cleaning his gun
how he missed family, especially me and mum.

Ended with love and kisses, I clear the cups and then
try to guess, what's beneath the bits,
blacked out by the censor's pen.
Mum re-folds the letter, eyes glistened moist with tears
shed for the man she hadn't seen, in four long lonely years.

Now I've lived a long life and made up my mind
that the world is a constant production line,
of babies, some bouncing their future assured,
a few arrive faulty, racked with pain
bearing the sins, still taking the blame
from a past indiscrete libertine's, moment of shame

born to die young, a few years of age
the ink barely dried, on the church registry page.

Naturally selected, the healthy ones then
go on to accomplish, their three scores and ten.
Husbands, mothers, siblings and others
aunties, uncles, the rich on the hill
lowly of the station, or ruling a nation.
When all's said and done, they're just "grist t' mill."

The last generation fought and died for their nation
and from war-weary Europe, a bloody gestation
produced hope in the shape of a new federation
to lessen the chance of new wars and their cause,
freedom of movement on borderless shores
But memory short, war forgotten, outdated,
short-sighted fools, rising rampant with hatred
vote to destroy the goodwill created
internet xenophobes express extreme views
poisoning minds with misleading news
screaming for all but indigenous Brits
to pack their bags, exit the doors
from recurrent hostile, once-welcoming shores.

Raised voices in violent discourse
splits divides and trends
towards argument between family
resentment in faithful old friends.

> Conducted by blinkered resurgent,
> ignorance once again roars
> retrospectively, for the emergence
> of perfection without any flaws
> a eugenically bred, fair of head
> Imperial conquering force.

When war was eventually declared I was fortunate to have been nine years old, an age mercifully when kids are lacking in worldly experience and aware only of their own personal selfish needs no matter how petty. At that period my mind was totally insulated against any sort of sympathy towards others no matter how great a trauma they may have suffered. I was, I suppose too young as yet to have developed an empathic side to my character, and mentally incapable of expressing sympathy for others in their hour of grief.

My mother for instance.

I didn't realise the amount of stress she suffered, the years of separation from Dad along with the worry for his safety, which manifested itself in the nervous rash lasting the rest of her life. During the nights spent in Aunty Nell's air raid shelter during the blitz, Grandma could be heard from next door in Aunty Elsie's shelter, hysterically crying above the cacophony of anti-aircraft fire and exploding bombs.

While I lay drowsily unperturbed gazing at the flickering candle's ever-widening sooty stain on the concrete ceiling.

Christmas Eve, 1944, I'm almost fifteen, Hitler has a last go at the Manchester area launching V1 flying bombs from over the North Sea, most explode harmlessly over a wide area, but one lands in Oldham killing nearly forty civilians just weeks away from the end of hostilities.

My first shot of adrenalin had arrived with empathy close on its heels.

5

The transmitting of hysteria by way of poetry in the hands, say of an unsuccessful writer, mind twisted with years of failure and bent on revenge against audiences skinny with the kudos, could have a devastating effect on the behaviour of gatherings large and small. My next piece describes the possible consequences.

A POEM OF MASS DESTRUCTION

We walk through life on our chosen track
to influence our peers, make an indelible impact
My ambition as a poet is to write and persistently dwell
on soul-destroying stanzas that over and over regaled
will convince the listening audience how horribly they've
failed.

In the beer-fumed friendly ambience
of the pub on a warm Sunday Night
deserved success will be mine at last, here on the open mic.
With an air of supreme confidence
giving it my very best go
smiling faces crumble to the pessimistic flow.

The audience sitting mesmerised is putty in my palm
little do they realise there's malice in my charm
I could tell from long drawn faces, unsmiling and morose
the climax to my solo spot was coming to a close.

Fulfilment of the master plan, this fanatical ambition
delivery of the final line brings my life's work to fruition
swaying uncontrollably, the crowd as one react
by jumping out the window
spellbound in a suicide pact.

Revenge is so sweet. After years of ridicule meted out by unappreciative morons who could never recognise a natural genius. My only personal disappointment suffered on the night was, having to cut the evening short thus saving the assembled, doomed, cultureless, punters further expense at the bar of this fantastically, depressing, astronomically high-priced, colourless venue.

The transmitting of hysteria by way of poetry in the hands,
say of an unsuccessful writer, mind twisted with years of
failure and bent on revenge against audiences skinny with
the kudos, could have a devastating effect on the behaviour
of gatherings large and small. My next piece describes the
possible consequences.

A POEM OF MASS DESTRUCTION

We walk through life on our chosen track
try to influence each other, make an indelible impact
My ambition as a poet is to write and persistently dwell

on wretched miserable stanzas that over and over regaled
will convince the listening punters how horribly they've failed.

In the beer-fumed friendly ambience
of the Baum on a warm Sunday Night
deserved success will be mine at last... here on the open mic.
With an air of supreme confidence... I give it my best go
smiling faces crumble to the pessimistic flow.
The audience sitting mesmerised is putty in my palm
little do they realise there's malice in my charm
I could tell from long drawn faces, unsmiling and morose
the climax to my solo spot... was coming to a close.

Fulfilment of the master plan, this fanatical ambition
triggered by the final line... brings my life's work to fruition
swaying uncontrollably... the crowd as one react
by jumping out the window... spellbound in a suicide pact.

The transmitting of hysteria by way of poetry in the hands,
say of an unsuccessful writer, mind twisted with years of
failure and bent on revenge against audiences skinny with
the kudos, could have a devastating effect on the behaviour
of gatherings large and small. My next piece describes the
possible consequences.

A POEM OF MASS DESTRUCTION

We walk through life on our chosen track
try to influence each other, make an indelible impact
My ambition as a poet is to write and persistently dwell
on wretched miserable stanzas that over and over regaled
will convince the listening punters how horribly they've
failed.

In the beer-fumed friendly ambience
of the Baum on a warm Sunday Night
deserved success will be mine at last... here on the open
mic.
With an air of supreme confidence... I give it my best go
smiling faces crumble to the pessimistic flow.
The audience sitting mesmerised is putty in my palm
little do they realise there's malice in my charm
I could tell from long drawn faces, unsmiling and morose
the climax to my solo spot... was coming to a close.

Fulfilment of the master plan, this fanatical ambition
triggered by the final line... brings my life's work to fruition
swaying uncontrollably... the crowd as one react
by jumping out the window... spellbound in a suicide pact.

Of an unsuccessful writer, mind twisted with years of failure
and bent on revenge against audiences skinny with the
kudos, could have a devastating effect on the behaviour of
gatherings large and small. My next piece describes the
possible consequences.

A POEM OF MASS DESTRUCTION

We walk through life on our chosen track
try to influence each other, make an indelible impact.
My ambition as a poet is to write and persistently dwell
on wretched miserable stanzas that over and over regaled
will convince the listening punters how horribly they've
failed.

In the beer-fumed friendly ambience
of the Baum on a warm Sunday Night
deserved success will be mine at last… here on the open
mic.
With an air of supreme confidence… I give it my best go
smiling faces crumble to the pessimistic flow.
The audience sitting mesmerised is putty in my palm
little do they realise there's malice in my charm
I could tell from long drawn faces, unsmiling and morose
the climax to my solo spot… was coming to a close.

Fulfilment of the master plan, this fanatical ambition
triggered by the final line… brings my life's work to fruition
swaying uncontrollably… the crowd as one react
by jumping out the window… spellbound in a suicide pact.

The transmitting of hysteria by way of poetry in the hands,
say of an unsuccessful writer, mind twisted with years of
failure and bent on revenge against audiences skinny with
the kudos, could have a devastating effect on the behaviour
of gatherings large and small. My next piece describes the
possible consequences.

A POEM OF MASS DESTRUCTION

We walk through life on our chosen track
try to influence each other, make an indelible impact.
My ambition as a poet is to write and persistently dwell
on wretched miserable stanzas that over and over regaled
will convince the listening punters how horribly they've
failed.

In the beer-fumed friendly ambience
of the Baum on a warm Sunday Night
deserved success will be mine at last… here on the open
mic.
With an air of supreme confidence… I give it my best go
smiling faces crumble to the pessimistic flow.
The audience sitting mesmerised is putty in my palm
little do they realise there's malice in my charm
I could tell from long drawn faces, unsmiling and morose
the climax to my solo spot… was coming to a close.

Fulfilment of the master plan, this fanatical ambition
triggered by the final line… brings my life's work to fruition
swaying uncontrollably… the crowd as one react
by jumping out the window… spellbound in a suicide pact.

The transmitting of hysteria by way of poetry in the hands,
say of an unsuccessful writer, mind twisted with years of
failure and bent on revenge against audiences skinny with
the kudos, could have a devastating effect on the behaviour
of gatherings large and small. My next piece describes the
possible consequences.

A POEM OF MASS DESTRUCTION

We walk through life on our chosen track
try to influence each other, make an indelible impact.
My ambition as a poet is to write and persistently dwell
on wretched miserable stanzas that over and over regaled
will convince the listening punters how horribly they've
failed.

In the beer-fumed friendly ambience
of the Baum on a warm Sunday Night
deserved success will be mine at last... here on the open
mic.
With an air of supreme confidence... I give it my best go
smiling faces crumble to the pessimistic flow.
The audience sitting mesmerised is putty in my palm
little do they realise there's malice in my charm
I could tell from long drawn faces, unsmiling and morose
the climax to my solo spot... was coming to a close.

Fulfilment of the master plan, this fanatical ambition
triggered by the final line... bring.
The transmitting of hysteria by way of poetry in the hands.

The transmitting of hysteria by way of poetry in the hands,
say of an unsuccessful writer, mind twisted with years of
failure and bent on revenge against audiences skinny with
the kudos, could have a devastating effect on the behaviour
of gatherings large and small. My next piece describes the
possible consequences.

A POEM OF MASS DESTRUCTION

We walk through life on our chosen track
try to influence each other, make an indelible impact.
My ambition as a poet is to write and persistently dwell
on wretched miserable stanzas that over and over regaled
will convince the listening punters how horribly they've
failed.

In the beer-fumed friendly ambience
of the Baum on a warm Sunday Night
deserved success will be mine at last… here on the open
mic.
With an air of supreme confidence… I give it my best go
smiling faces crumble to the pessimistic flow.
The audience sitting mesmerised is putty in my palm
little do they realise there's malice in my charm
I could tell from long drawn faces, unsmiling and morose
the climax to my solo spot… was coming to a close.

Fulfilment of the master plan, this fanatical ambition
triggered by the final line… brings my life's work to fruition
swaying uncontrollably… the crowd as one react
by jumping out the window… spellbound in a suicide pact.

The transmitting of hysteria by way of poetry in the hands,
say of an unsuccessful writer, mind twisted with years of
failure and bent on revenge against audiences skinny with
the kudos, could have a devastating effect on the behaviour
of gatherings large and small. My next piece describes the
possible consequences.

A POEM OF MASS DESTRUCTION

We walk through life on our chosen track
try to influence each other, make an indelible impact.
My ambition as a poet is to write and persistently dwell
on wretched miserable stanzas that over and over regaled
will convince the listening punters how horribly they've
failed.

In the beer-fumed friendly ambience
of the Baum on a warm Sunday Night
deserved success will be mine at last... here on the open
mic.
With an air of supreme confidence... I give it my best go
smiling faces crumble to the pessimistic flow.
The audience sitting mesmerised is putty in my palm
little do they realise there's malice in my charm
I could tell from long drawn faces, unsmiling and morose
the climax to my solo spot... was coming to a close.

Fulfilment of the master plan, this fanatical ambition
triggered by the final line... brings my life's work to fruition
swaying uncontrollably... the crowd as one react
by jumping out the window... spellbound in a suicide pact.

The transmitting of hysteria by way of poetry in the hands,
say of an unsuccessful writer, mind twisted with years of
failure and bent on revenge against audiences skinny with
the kudos, could have a devastating effect on the behaviour
of gatherings large and small. My next piece describes the
possible consequences.

A POEM OF MASS DESTRUCTION

We walk through life on our chosen track
try to influence each other, make an indelible impact.
My ambition as a poet is to write and persistently dwell
on wretched miserable stanzas that over and over regaled
will convince the listening punters how horribly they've
failed.

In the beer-fumed friendly ambience
of the Baum on a warm Sunday Night
deserved success will be mine at last… here on the open
mic.
With an air of supreme confidence… I give it my best go
smiling faces crumble to the pessimistic flow.
The audience sitting mesmerised is putty in my palm
little do they realise there's malice in my charm
I could tell from long drawn faces, unsmiling and morose
the climax to my solo spot… was coming to a close.

Fulfilment of the master plan, this fanatical ambition
triggered by the final line… brings my life's work to fruition
swaying uncontrollably… the crowd as one react
by jumping out the window… spellbound in a suicide pact.

Of an unsuccessful writer, mind twisted with years of failure
and bent on revenge against audiences skinny with the
kudos, could have a devastating effect on the behaviour of
gatherings large and small. My next piece describes the
possible consequences.

A POEM OF MASS DESTRUCTION

We walk through life on our chosen track
try to influence each other, make an indelible impact.
My ambition as a poet is to write and persistently dwell
on wretched miserable stanzas that over and over regaled
will convince the listening punters how horribly they've failed.

In the beer-fumed friendly ambience
of the Baum on a warm Sunday Night
deserved success will be mine at last... here on the open mic.
With an air of supreme confidence... I give it my best go
smiling faces crumble to the pessimistic flow.
The audience sitting mesmerised is putty in my palm
little do they realise there's malice in my charm
I could tell from long drawn faces, unsmiling and morose
the climax to my solo spot... was coming to a close.

Fulfilment of the master plan, this fanatical ambition
triggered by the final line... brings my life's work to fruition
swaying uncontrollably... the crowd as one react
by jumping out the window... spellbound in a suicide pact.

The transmitting of hysteria by way of poetry in the hands,
say of an unsuccessful writer, mind twisted with years of
failure and bent on revenge against audiences skinny with
the kudos, could have a devastating effect on the behaviour
of gatherings large and small. My next piece describes the
possible consequences.

A POEM OF MASS DESTRUCTION

We walk through life on our chosen track
try to influence each other, make an indelible impact.
My ambition as a poet is to write and persistently dwell
on wretched miserable stanzas that over and over regaled
will convince the listening punters how horribly they've failed.

In the beer-fumed friendly ambience
of the Baum on a warm Sunday Night
deserved success will be mine at last... here on the open mic.
With an air of supreme confidence... I give it my best go
smiling faces crumble to the pessimistic flow.
The audience sitting mesmerised is putty in my palm
little do they realise there's malice in my charm
I could tell from long drawn faces, unsmiling and morose
the climax to my solo spot... was coming to a close.

Fulfilment of the master plan, this fanatical ambition
triggered by the final line... brings my life's work to fruition
swaying uncontrollably... the crowd as one react
by jumping out the window... spellbound in a suicide pact.

The transmitting of hysteria by way of poetry in the hands,
say of an unsuccessful writer, mind twisted with years of
failure and bent on revenge against audiences skinny with
the kudos, could have a devastating effect on the behaviour
of gatherings large and small. My next piece describes the
possible consequences.

A POEM OF MASS DESTRUCTION

We walk through life on our chosen track
try to influence each other, make an indelible impact.
My ambition as a poet is to write and persistently dwell
on wretched miserable stanzas that over and over regaled
will convince the listening punters how horribly they've
failed.

In the beer-fumed friendly ambience
of the Baum on a warm Sunday Night
deserved success will be mine at last… here on the open
mic.
With an air of supreme confidence… I give it my best go
smiling faces crumble to the pessimistic flow.
The audience sitting mesmerised is putty in my palm
little do they realise there's malice in my charm
I could tell from long drawn faces, unsmiling and morose
the climax to my solo spot… was coming to a close.

Fulfilment of the master plan, this fanatical ambition
triggered by the final line… brings my life's work to
fruition.
Swaying uncontrollably… the crowd as one react
by jumping out the window… spellbound in a suicide pact.

Every year after the party season people use the beginning of
this period as an easy-to-remember starting point from
which they've pledged to banish an accumulation of dodgy
vices, life-threatening or otherwise, out of their everyday

existence. But with very few lacking the determination to see them through.
This poem contrary to the usual outcome is the story of one middle-aged individual scared into success.

NEW YEAR RESOLUTIONS

Christmas over, good cheer gone stale
cause and effect drinking beer by the pail
cards with good wishes still lie on the mat
can't pick them up, am too f'kin fat.

Sluggish lethargic toxin polluted
oversized arse in the armchair well rooted
from high-flying flows to miserable ebbs
smell like a vat of, last New Year Eve's dreggs.

Feel rough in the morning sickly and pale
letterbox rattles with incoming mail
shaven, showered, heaved myself on the scale
a peep over stomach brings a pitiful moan
read out announces, eighteen 'n' half stone.
Impressive, imposing, when one's six foot three
barrel of lard, if you're short arsed like me.

Really went over the top last year
abused me with all sorts of gear
to get back in shape, an inexpensive solution
I tried an intensive, New Year resolution
it's for a long time, and I'm not all that keen.
But been told if I don't.

"Won't see Christmas Eighteen"
Enrolled at the Gym and waddling in
introduce me to Stan "the man with a plan"
to eradicate poundage, get back fit and thin
starts in with a pep talk, "So important to win"
catalogues fat bits, and when to begin.

Quarter pound ear lobes, eyes sunken and hid
to expose each again needs a lipo-sucked lid.
It takes twelve months, on salads and gherkins
to restore firm flat six-packs
from nine-gallon firkins.
Determined, single-minded,
strict adherence, to instruction
will invigorate vitality
toned muscle construction.

Thank God it's over, wasn't much fun
tempting smells from the chippie
I'd resisted and won
I've lost so much weight, I'm in fact really thin
through unstinting hard graft, and willpower
and to stay this way, exercise every day
Running round.
To get wet in the shower.

A threat to one's health caused by excesses of the good things in life is the inescapable make your mind up time as to your future choice of lifestyle. Will it be the short sweet continuation of the "Have a nice day keep the bed sores away" Early Death Bed Plan? Overweight riddled with type 2 diabetes.

Or the long (Healthy Decline Plan) alternative, "With more springs to enjoy" But unlike the short-term plan. This one comes with an extra time bonus to enjoy the sleepless nights plagued with worry regarding the dwindling sufficiency of your pension pot.

This is a sad tale concerning a young man without friends and the confidence to approach girls. Who after constant rejection by the opposite sex plans to kidnap then enslave one. But being shy, lacking in confidence, and afraid to carry out his plan. Vents his anger on an Internet downloaded, disembodied mechanical female voice. Alexa.

CLOSET MISOGYNIST

Girls snigger at each other, avoiding
my advances when I sidle up with outdated lines at the local disco dances. They think I'm a wimp,
an excruciating bore. Whirling around making shapes,
on the drink and sweat-stained floor. Disco finished, nearly dawn, down-hearted, despairing, feeling forlorn,
key opens the front door with a welcoming click, a quick glance in the mirror as I pass down the hall see me creased and untidy, don't resemble at all, that exuberant, vibrant, hunk of meat, who some hours before had took to the street.
looking for love to a garage-house beat
I'm not so good-looking, dim-witted, a bit thick,
and the chickens fell off my shish kabob stick.
Introverted, never been kissed, left off everyone's party list,
zero plus in self-esteem. And the buzz words used to

reference me on the bustling cool street scene, speak of an.
"Inexperienced no nothing lanky, Never had a girl, Gobshite Mancy."
In the face of such blatant disregard, I'm a furious hopeless contender, consumed with a nagging burning desire.
For revenge on the opposite gender.

So I Google Amazon, then hatch a plot, wire up the house with echo spots. And on starting my evil agenda,
throw the switch, the Apps spring to life. Enslaving that smug bitch Alexa. I begin with the tunes,
forty million all told, from one-hit wonders,
through to those that got gold. Elvis, Sinatra, old groaner Bing, Cliff Richard, new order, Dean Martin, and Sting. In quick succession I order her to play,
she's had no rest… at all, since yesterday.
But what's gone wrong, the plot's in crisis. It's me that's got the laryngitis.

I insult her, demean her, shriek that she's lazy,
neighbours must think I'm mad or gone crazy.
But she never ever fails to come back. Composed… fresh as a daisy.
Press on regardless not a minute respite, make her flush the bog, when I take a John Bright.

My constant reminder is, "Girls are incomplete males"
According to Aristotle. Finally flips her over the edge.
with gargantuan loss of her bottle. I've brought to cessation my burning obsession, having done a magnificent job.

I knew I was getting my own back when I sensed a
submissive sob. And to confirm this glorious victory
"elimination of irrational fears" was
the Echo spots silent and rusting in puddles. Of Alexa's
tears.

No longer afraid of women I'm a misogynist Mr Big.
A chest swollen proud to be ousted. Supremacist Chauvinist
PIG.

Did rich Brexiteers the likes of Jacob Reece Mogg put up a smoke-screen of "more money for the NHS to conceal the real motives for dumping the EU."

For instance, knowing Brexit would give them more opportunities for higher returns on their portfolio of investments, free from EU restriction? Give them also the opportunity of high returns, by asset stripping what would be newly deregulated EU protected areas of natural resources for short-term gain.

Should MPs be debarred from parliament for having industrial investments of any kind if those investments depend on Government influence for their prosperity?

Even royalty has or had money invested in the ruthless exploitive money lending (sharks) Brighter Homes, previously known as Crazy George furnishers, to partially maintain their luxury lifestyles from the obscene interest rates wrung from the poorest in British society, by way of the Brighter Homes rent to buy racket.

THE BREXIT BLUES

It's twenty-one months since the vote for autonomy
unentangling ourselves from the EU economy
free, at last, new trade deals to seek
plus saving one-third of a billion each week
a brilliant future together we face
on a 20% meagre, industrial base?

Cheap goods come and go on Korean-made shipping
Footsie one hundred's sky high and no dipping
raising false hope, for sustained prosperity.
Imports are paid for in shrinking assets
and "hired out" numeric dexterity.

Alongside cooking the company books, for conglomerate grandees
we sell our unique world-renowned, financial expertise
to oppressive corrupt governments in power overseas.
Charity turned to dollars for exceptionally large fees.
Then have them re-invest it into pre-assigned devices
selling chunks of London off to criminal franchises.
Many of whom have shady links
arming the murderous ISIS.

Monies stolen from funding,
intended to soothe third world pain.
Shows up returned, as an honest earned?
above-board, Market gain.

Some of these gangsters buy football clubs
and are really well established
living abroad, leading luxury lives
chauffeurs and flunkies serve glamorous wives.
Running ill-gotten empires, with emails and faxes.
It's champagne each day, leaving us here to pay.
The shortfall in lost UK taxes.

World's away from their countrymen's plight,
the diseased, unemployed, food famished.
Money donated, for the poor of all ages
crookedly cleaned in a series of stages.
Finds its way back to pay footballers wages.

From the trillions distributed around the world
we see a scandalous painting unfurled
entitled THEFT OF FUNDS AWARDED.
Millions lavished on real estate
and Premier League centre forwards.

Britain's "We Do All The Currencies"
slick Financial Team
the metaphorical only one made, "British washing machine"
will launder your money as a matter of course
clean like a whistle, no paper-trailed source.
Strong plastic tenners and rubbery fivers
guarantee us top-placed "Free Market" survivors.

The decision to leave Europe, in panic-stricken haste
was not from careful reasoning, but intolerance of race
It will take a generation to revive our failing nation

recover from the consequence of, rash voting's devastation.
Plus innumerable anomalies will show as wasted time
during which there's likely to be
runaway inflation… instability.
No money left in the Chancellors' purse
bogged down, derailed, offline,
Let's face it folks there's no plan B.
We've advanced the west's decline.

Since I've written the above despairing whine, my respect for the British establishment especially the managers of its MPs (Manipulative Pricks) has plunged to a dangerous level after watching our unscripted leaders on TV appearing to not quite know what they were talking about when competing for the vacant Prime Ministership. As noisy confused argument supported with lots of arm waving, degenerated into (can't think of anything to say) silent arm waving, we the watching public suddenly realised, these clowns are no better than us, that we need to stay in the EU and hope against hope being lost in a larger assembly might eventually encourage our lot to piss facing in the same direction as Angela Mertle, to the strains of "Ode To Joy."

6

Tears can have far-reaching effects, even for those lucky
enough not to have been emotionally affected by the death
of a close relative in times of war.
This poem besides being just another angle on remembrance
day, exposes the possible consequential years of
unhappiness on marrying the recently war widowed.

YOU'RE NOT HALF THE MAN HE WAS

At the eleventh hour, on the eleventh day,
of the eleventh month, in a mournful array
under skeletal trees, on last summer's leaf
thousands of faces, in sombre relief
display circumstantially, countenanced grief.

Lugubrious music will coax mouths to pray
round a poppy-strewn plinth at eleven today
and honour by way of a well-worn agender
a body count up since a year last November.

Contrived euphemistic rhetoric
amplified from a mitred head
conjures up a mental picture,
of smiley faces on the dead.

Imploring us to remember, in two short minutes recall,
heroes who suffered the ultimate, sacrificed their all.
Inclusive of those, who raped, ravaged,
killed innocent kids, via collateral damage.

The winds of time sighing by,
first cool, stem, then gently dry
tear-stained cheeks, sore widowed eyes.

She watches TV, "remarried"
heart scarred, but with time will repair,
devoted second husband
ill at ease in his favourite chair
feels resurgent annual jealousy
seeing tears she cannot hide
for her posthumous soldier first love,
cruelly denied.

He waits and hopes fading memory
will stop, then dry falling tears
bring to an end the mourning
blighting their union's first years.
As the flames carried high for her hero
flicker then finally dim
she might unlock the door to his love with her heart
at last, devoted to him.

History tells me that all wars are completely unnecessary as their final results definitely do not justify the huge financial outlay involved, or the devastating incalculable human suffering of idiots marching to their deaths, singing "I've got sixpence" after assuring loved ones confidently that "it'll be all over by Christmas."

7

Being born is a most traumatic experience. Pulled and pushed into a cruel world of exploitation. A world where from day one in order to survive, we have to spend each twenty-four hour period being hardened off and desensitised tackling the innumerable daily challenges thrown up as we stumble through this euphemistically disguised vale of tears. On the difficult to navigate. Yellow brick road to experience.

IT'S A WONDERFUL WORLD (OR IS IT?)

In a tiny corner of the Milky Way
just before dawn at the break of the day
inside a room under star-lit skies
lubricated by blood to loud agonised cries
I'm pushed into hell
from between Mother's thighs.

Torture is harsh and immediate
at such a tender age
as the Midwife slashes my lifeline, in a gory second stage
Mum's nine months of discomfort
forgotten with a sigh

burly woman in uniform
clears my mouth and makes me cry.

It was SO comfy in Mummies womb
plenty to eat with bags of room
then loosed like a hound from life's starting trap
to the human race, on my very first lap.

Christened in church, a miserable place
strange man sloshes water all over my face
while going on about some God "in his grace."

At last, it's over tears are dried
Mum's thumb in my mouth smiling with pride
glasses clinking, my frightened eyes blinking
all attending their wonder
what I must be thinking.

Wake early the next morning not at all happy
crying my eyes out wearing a soggy wet nappy
bathed, cleansed, sweet powdered posterior
ready for jabbing, against mumps and diphtheria.

Totally dependent, the first few miles
in a haphazard world full of paedophile's
pain a plenty awaits me anon
between my constant enquiries
as to where I came from?

The year's march on one by one
some remembered with tears when their parents passed on
their batons of wisdom for daughter and son
to improve on wise sayings left in their wake
"resist getting angry" if kids irritate
ignore you when speaking, break the odd plate
and if disrespectful they answer you back,
respond with a hug don't give them a slap
they need love and patience, for as long as it takes
on the long road to wisdom
paved with first-time mistakes.

Life's bad enough so don't be divisive
as do terrorists, keep our country in crisis
innocents killed by the black-hearted ISIS!
uneasy truce with the IRA!
man stabbed to death in bar room affray!
each hour's filled with bad news, day after day.

If you're lucky or otherwise to have lived a long life
struggled to get through the sadness and strife
scarred by illness, survived surgeon's knife
repaid the mortgage, buried your wife.

Is there really this forgiving host
up there with son Christ, and a Holy Ghost
to greet me beyond the finishing post?
I can't be sure I'm hard to convince
that we'll share the same Heaven, a peasant with prince
I refuse to believe it and with certainty guess
if there is such a place

we'll surely arrive, for him to assess
unhinged by gross horrors and traumatic stress
It's almost over, I've had some good runs
as a devout non-believer I'll stick to my guns.
'cos I firmly believe after popping your clogs
there's no such a place where a God catalogues
only we humans, not insects and frogs.

Life concluded, over and done
remembered with love by daughter and son
then forgotten completely
when they're passed and gone.

Together at peace all the family dead
on top of each other like in a bunk bed.
Ran the race, did the best I could
an out of the betting also ran
it doesn't matter everyone wins
absolute absolution, no matter their sins.

The good are quickly forgotten
along with their different days
the bad long remembered legends
for their wicked nefarious ways.
Lie where the sands of time
part to embrace, cracked blistered foot
tired wrinkled face.

Don't worry about hearing the starters gun
for a winning rosette's pinned to everyone.
On reaching the peace that's Oblivion.

Well as you've probably gathered after reading that, I'm not one for piety in any way, although I was in the early years given quite a thorough grounding by my dear mother in the protocol of church procedure. I also vividly remember the ritual bedtime prayers with me and my older brother kneeling on either side of the chamber pot hands clasped together, eyes tight shut, asking God to bless by name each and every member of the family, which took a quite considerable time.

8

This poem illustrates the dangers to the newly born of a window left open in a labour ward, especially at daybreak.
First impression syndrome
Or the young duck effect.
Mum and Dad were so excited, that early April morn
by the arrival of another son, their second-to-be-born
every bird residing, on this half of our blacked-out sphere
sits waiting in good vantage, silent on a tree
to welcome one more infant day
and coincidentally "me"
the rising sun creeps into the room
chasing away, stale colourless gloom
Cloud-flickered sun-sent golden rays, miles in millions long
raise the heads of dormant life, rouse sleepy birds to song.

Un-comfy on the baby scale, I begin to whimper, whinge and wail
but being born at the break of the day
in the last few hours of April, just before the first of May
immediately I'm aware of through an open window, amplified.
A cacophony of whistling by a host of birds outside

indelibly imprints, onto my tiny little mind
All about were giggling, as I chirruped in distress
stern faceted ward Sister, standing stiffly in a starched dress
gropes for a rational reason with an educated guess
"There is recorded evidence," said she
and continued, deeply thinking
recalled from the past a similar event, via the vaguest of inkling
That. "The birthday sign of Taurus is a logical reason for us
to not expect of the thousands born
everyone to be perfect and flawless.
A few could be influenced, nay, scarred for life!
interrupting, a heightened dawn chorus."
Back home now, Mum works a routine

into which we quickly settle
for I was an awkward baby built,
for the testing of parental mettle.
Dad searches walls, woken yet again
for the nursery light at 2:30 am.

Not summoned by a human
what you'd call conventional sob
more akin, to a bubbling kettle
whistling on the hob.

I ascribe my notoriety
to an eclectic bunch of tuneful friends
in thousands of different varieties.
Parliaments of owls, covers of coots,
doles of white doves, a building of rooks

living and laying, eggs in spring nests,
farmers consider some, serious pests.

Most can fly free, as do you and me
sharing the sunshine with insects and bees
robins and sparrows abound in small lots
thousands of starlings murmurate in large flocks,
others in cages, singing songs looking pretty.
Little or fat, blue green or black.
The family word when referring to each bird
is the colloquial prefix of
"Dicky."

This tragic event you have just related to yourself was one of the worst health and safety risks to have gone unanticipated during the formative years of the newly created N H S handpicked anomaly spotting team, recently redundant from Bletchley Health, after the cessation of World War II hostilities. No more information, because of its sensitivity, can be released. All whistle-blowers will be dealt with severely.

9

This poem is dedicated to Tony Naylor who once lived in our Sheltered Scheme and whom I never saw with anything other than a smile on his face (till now?) Though I'm sure knowing what a gentle soul he was wouldn't take exception to this light-hearted biography of himself.

THE GOOD LIFE

A neighbour of mine aged ninety-three
of whom many friends concurred to agree
no nicer guy could there ever be
devoted Christian, his everyday function
was surrogate Pope in Middleton Junction
walked to Church up to three times a day
assisted priests in every which way
counted out biscuits and shots for communion
washed sinks full of pots, from last night's Mother's Union
this good kind gentle God-phile, altruistic nature
prayed nonstop for his fellow men, the sinful ones as well as
God (he hoped) was grateful, for his work up there in
Heaven.

On his knees from dawn till night, inclusive twenty-
four/seven

Came a time when he fell gravely ill
beyond the help of a doctor or pill
pale of face through cracked dry lips
kin gathered heard him say
"Throughout ninety years of devotion
and time spent as an amateur Lay
I've served the Lord unerring, all my life and still
accept this dreaded moment, to be God almighty's will."
The workman-like Priest mutters quietly, last rites in a
repetitive way
scatters a few drops of water, for a life completed that day.

God meanwhile in Heaven
phoned his Pope at the Holy See,
declaring
"I'll have to watch it in future
this guy's more religious than me"
he simply oozes goodness and is likely in future to be
a worrying threat to the prospects, of our Trinity's Gang of
Three
he's a hater of globalisation, our progress to world
integration
and worst of all I hear
wants restrictions on other than British up here
his articulate cunning rhetoric, to gullible throats, brings a
lump
puts me in mind of that carrot-topped twat
misogynist Donald Trump

So if you're looking for contentment on eventual demise
it's like going down to the woods today
you're in for a big surprise.
If there really is a Heaven, the existing backside of the sun
don't believe in all that hearsay
a new regimes begun
God's been deposed, in a Coup de ta.
Now our Tony's Cock 'O' The Run.

Tony was really born in God's image, my opinion tells me he was an identical clone quite capable I bet, of sending plagues down, but not the malicious get-your-own-back sort. Take for instance if the proper god had infected all his children with carbuncles, Tony as vice God would have immediately blanketed the Earth with a bread poultice despite the certainty of having to face his master in full wrath later. How good is that?

10

This is a pre-Christmas poem recalling when our Great Britain ruled one-fifth of the earth together with a third of it's population and all the sea's surrounding everywhere else. When life for the ruling class was an overflowing cornucopia of excess and you got four dollars to the pound. But mercifully short for the deprived stunted working class majority at the far extreme of the social divide.

Has there really been a recession since 2008? (never noticed it myself).

HARD TIMES

When the man of the house in the old days
either died or lost his job,
his dependents were put in the workhouse
or went thieving to make a few bobs.

The same thing happened to our dad,
turned up drunk and got sacked from the Mill
but life didn't appeal in the workhouse
separation was part of the drill

so instead we were taken in by Granddad
Son Fred and his wife Aunty Jill.

On arriving that day late at Grandpa's
Mum tearfully said with a frown,
it's going to be a bit of a squeeze
in a tiny two up and two down.

This is no time for tears now dear Daughter,
said her dad on the dust-covered floor,
when the Cockroaches saw you lot coming
they packed up and moved in next door.

There wasn't much room to begin with
especially time for bed,
Mum and the girls shared with Aunty Jill.
While I squeezed in between Grandpa,
me Dad and sweaty feet Fred.

Choking fog, diphtheria,
curtains and beds, bug-infested,
complicate life even more so,
on top of being born pigeon-chested.

Everyone self-medicated
with dubious potions to treat,
dozens of different ailments
in efforts to gain some relief,
from the perils of everyday problems
soothing the redness and pain
inflicted on us by our Teacher

with his long thick black knobbly cane
One of the cures for example,
viewed now with some disbelief
was a daily teaspoon of water
in which Grandma had soaked her false teeth.
The provenance supporting this treatment
with the passage of time is obscure
but we think we now have the answer,
It's an immune-supporting cure
only effective if carefully made
from a God-fearing, aged mature.

These days when we die, are much better,
you're frozen till there's a day,
they find a cure for whatever.
Killed and made you that way.

Now if given that choice when I was a boy
I would've been "put down" and froze,
to await better times like Christmas
for a motive quite odd you'd suppose.
When we'd each and all, get a large chicken leg,
instead of the Parson's nose.

There's at least one consultative fact to having lived in those hard times, and that was to be thankful for not having been born a hundred years earlier. Or today.

Have you Sinners noticed though, that God through his kindness made it so that the harder life is. The shorter it will be.

Hallelujah!

11

This is my personal tribute, and I'm sure the rest of
Middletonians will endorse the sentiment expressed.
To a team of unpaid volunteers who after months of hard
graft have gradually transformed the Borough's grot spots
with triumphal culmination. From "Ugly OURS IS A NICE
TOWN OURS IS Ducklings" to "Beautiful Swans."

In a council community building
next door to the hare and hounds pub
therein gathers a group of Middleton-philes
assembled to do the town good.

After a two- to three-hour gestation
seeded by everyone there,
came a smiling pronouncement from Paula
in her capacity as chair
that tonight on this cold winter evening
a unanimous vote in the room
had welcomed the newly born healthy.
Middleton Borough in bloom.

Tracey and Jan on the council's behalf
pledge their whole-hearted support
while Pat and Lisa's, Saint Martins Gang
just give it a little more thought.

Davina, speaks to Keeley
in convivial light rapport.
benignly watched over by Vicar,
the Reverend Martin Short.

Volunteers, Ros, Jan, and Zoe,
Catlin, Chris, and Tom
Impatiently wait for springtime.
Can't wait to get it on.

Jill of Youth Liaison,
as soon as the meeting ends
takes written notes from the minutes
to impact on her immature friends.

Heather together with Julie
concentrating with eager intent
listen to Lee, the purser
guesstimating the cash to be spent.

It's now high summer we're rushing around
unprecedented sunshine bakes the ground
everyone frantically on the go
reviving plants with H_2O.

Anomalous pressures to cope with,
by far exceed one or two.
Then there's World War I anniversary
Have we bitten off, too much to chew?

It's not all the time easy going
the path's been occasionally rocky,
stumbling over minor disputes
like for instance the Hanson Street poppy.
Lifting rubbish from gum-poc-marked paving
till late in the afternoon
perspiring profusely about the Borough,
under a merciless sun since June.
As cigarette ends quickly pile up
on the footpath without Wetherspoons.

Our mission is nearing completion
and the resultant social cohesion
saw the magnificent barge at Slattocks
sail in for its first summer season.

Beautiful floral features
hang from Pubs, cafes, and Inns
along squeaky clean environs
absent of wheelie bins.

It's getting close to judgement day
when adjudicators,
touring the town will say
does it deserving a yay or nay.

> A miserable nay, or an excellent yay
> will be met in an equivalent way
> with unanimous empathic humour.
> So no matter the outcome
> let's have three great big cheers.
> for the ubiquitous
> Middleton bloomers.

If you don't already know, Middleton is a small town in a huge conurbation insulated between Manchester Oldham and Rochdale by an ever-decreasing green belt slowly vanishing under developments of unwanted warehousing and industrial sites doomed to lie vacant like the ones from a previous age. This is why 'logically thinking' Middleton In Bloom was created to compensate in some way for the loss of the natural boundary, by moving it into the streets with some success as the past two years have shown, a silver medal was awarded with our first effort in 2017, then last year 2018, silver guilt. This year. Who knows? Onward and upward. Middleton is unique in that twice a year the homeless hold a flag day for us.

> This is a modern version of the fairy tale about the wicked
> old fairy who put a curse on the king's newborn baby
> daughter because she wasn't invited to the do.

> Which resulted in the princess and her whole court having a
> hundred-year kip until a handsome young prince came along
> awakening her with a kiss and claiming her as his bride.

Whether they lived "Happy ever after" or not, I don't know,
because in this version their initial beginnings contrary to the
original story were quite embarrassing.

I'll spare you the first part of the story, and we find the
prince approaching the princess's overgrown castle.

The brambles parted the prince upped and started,
towards the castle door
Glancing back had a panic attack
tempered with sweaty palm fear
as the re-growing thicket and slumbering pickets
de-chanced a retreat to the rear.

Furtively creeping by fast-asleep servants,
and comatose palace guards,
mutters,
"this fairy tale method of finding a partner"
is intensive and so very hard
Was alright I suppose, in the days of old
when knights were bold
and computers, a far-off invention.
"Remember" to update the Monarchy
was one of the old king's intention
So going online will be simple and fine
a fat equerry butts in to mention.

There are huge selections… in the "Date a Bird" sections.
With girls of a mind, optimistic to find
something better than… poor peasant grafters.
Dreaming all day they'll be carried away

By a "well-minted" prince
'swhat they're after.

I'll do that anon, but for now, carry on
said he with unwavering duty
and on lifting the latch… his breath he did catch
at the sight of this sleeping beauty.

An attendant advisor,
helped take off his visor
as he got himself down on one knee
and with lips puckered up… to steal a kiss
thought… why not a couple, or three?

But after the first… her eyes opened wide
looked at her suitor… and through running tears cried
"I'm distressed and cannot reciprocate"
as I should… to your tender advances
for there's more than enough… other stuff on my mind
to indulge in your lust-provoked fancies.
Please forgive… if I seem disrespectful
bordering on the remiss.
But I've just been asleep for the past hundred years.
"And" am bursting for a piss.

12

Living by one's self has its advantages, for instance, you have the unopposed power of pleasing yourself in whatever you do. In what could be described as a most delightful super selfish altruistic free zone.

There is though, the need for a high degree of relentless self-discipline to ensure and maintain acceptable standards, now that you have to iron your own shirts.

This is the story of one such person's successful resurrection after sliding down the "Can't be bothered" pit of degradation.

CLEAN AS A MAN CALLED DAVID

Stuck in the house it's Easter again
can't go out 'cos it's pouring with rain
skies clear up, rainbow brightens the day.
Dying April welcomes blossom-filled May.

Should I sit in the garden, or laze on the grass
take an excursion with my pensioners pass.
But the seats on the Metro, are too hard a ride
sod it I'll stay, and do nothing inside.

Air the bedroom and open the post
breakfast spent sucking at two rounds of toast
couldn't finish them off, fed pigeons the most.

Gummed down a bowl of Special K
pots in the sink, from a week yesterday
watch clouds re-gather, then randomly spray
oh what a miserable f'kin day
my pants need pressing; there's a hole in my shoe
hundreds of jobs, can't be bothered to do.

Am I getting scruffy
haven't shaved yet today
does it really matter?
don't get out much anyway.
Time to make my mind up
do I go, or should I stay?

Must admit I've neglected
the habitat where I dwell
Don't get as many visitors now
I wonder do I smell?

I'll have to get out of this rut I'm in
my muscles are gone, losing weight very thin
heart's palpitating, incontinent bladder
unnecessary useless
as a carpet fitter ladder
this rapid decline I must halt and contain
build up my body, and physique to regain

confidence, whatever, keep virile and sane.
I'm sure feeling better, is worth the pain.

The resultant reward, of running for fun
was the bolstered up cheeks, of my skeletal bum
a restless bundle of energy am I,
from ugly bug chrysalis to new butterfly
symbolic of power, in an athlete's vest
four inches off my stomach, transferred to my chest
not still for a minute, don't ever rest.

The bathroom is a temple
where I worked, achieving my goal
with exercise thorough but gentle
thrown out, all the cheap toilet rolls.
And Andrex has lately upgraded.
No longer pathetic and jaded
head held high, walking tall
velvety Andrex hangs on the lavatory wall.

Who'd have thought I could agree
that taking advice from a kid on TV
would bring such a change, stimulate me
this upright, virile, dissipate free
steely framed, muscle-bound, fit as a flea
de-clinkered, re-lifestyled, re-graded.
Bum Andrex polished, morphed into being
"Clean as a man called David."

The afore-written epos
is dedicated to
the Middleton in Bloomers
of whom there're but a few.
So if you want to swell their ranks
and add your talents NOW
Google Bloomers up, at Facebook
KaPOW KaPOW KaPOW!

13

YOU CAN'T PLEASE EVERYONE

On a rubbish-strewn corner of Middleton
armed with secateurs bin bags and broom
Ros and Jan clear litter
for this year's "Borough in Bloom."

Joined by enthused residents
refreshed with biscuits and tea
continue their voluntary clean-up
on behalf of you and me.

Uncovering an old rusting street sign
at the edge of the tidied plot
they thought.
It's a century gone since World War I
and in case we might've forgotten.

Ros. by way of her hobby
paints the sign a coat of white
emphasising a painted red poppy
to locals' and passers' delight.
This tiny colourful symbol

provokes passing minds to remember
the eleventh hour of the eleventh day
when they called a halt to that bloody affray.
One hundred years since
come November.

The people on Highways completely aghast
act out of character, very fast
circulating this round-robin copy
"If we can't get at them for breaking by-laws
we'll have them, for being too soppy."

Please!… leave the poppy, to its silent work
jogging present-day minds to remember.
Let it go on and flower
till the hundredth year's past
at the eleventh hour… Of the eleventh day
on that cool Autumn morn next November.

Councils are certainly not sentimental when it comes down to one-hundred-year anniversary remembrances as you will have gathered after reading of their dogged intransigence in refusing to bend slightly, a highway by-law, broken by accident because no one was aware of it anyway. Pity they don't react to public opinion as swiftly as parking tickets are metered out here.

"Rip 'Em Off" Rochdale

14

Reading this poem at my son's funeral was the most emotional and upsetting experience I've ever been tasked with.

MICHAEL

On a bright frosty day at Foxall Street,
early 1963
A child was born named Michael
to Margaret and me

Memories come flooding back
when the world was vibrant, alive
optimistic for the future
our family complete at five.

We'd already been blessed with two beautiful girls
but because of a pill,
his mum to be
"inadvertent" omitted to take.
Must admit now, that baby Michael
was a happy, but unplanned mistake

He hated school, loved riding in cars
an intense to frequent, pain in the arse.
But he settled down and finally found
through music, he could succeed
be an ace guitarist,
the very best of leads.

Spent hours alone self-teaching
by himself in long noisy sessions
mastered the art of music
unaided without any lessons.
At his ultimate peak of perfection
he travelled the world wide and far
to us, he was a legend
a brilliant shining star.

The last gig is over, the bright lights are dim
each one of us here will remember him.
He's played a last encore, for every fan
downed his pint, loaded the van
for the long journey home,
where you can,
rest easy tonight.
Mister music man.

Michael is my late son who provided me with the moment every parent dreads but does not expect. Dying before his time. Given the choice I would have preferred the short straw for myself, than suffer the heartache, a too-long life can bring.

15

You've all heard Shakespeare saying "The world is a stage"
on which we all briefly appear before moving on. This poem
is a whimsical summary of the events surrounding the
existence of a random group performing in the repetitive
play we call life.
Luckily being married to, and encouraged by his wife Anne,
Shakespeare became England's greatest writer Which begs
the question
Would he have been so successful had he been married to a
woman like Nora Batty
William Shakespeare died on 23 April 1616, aged 52.
52/2 = A pair of alphabets.

FIRST AND LAST NIGHT

To quote top playwright Will Shakespeare
remembered this four hundred years
from among his much hackneyed sayings
there's a couple that spring to mind here.
One's about Cleo's lover,
wanting to borrow his countrymen's ears.

And "The world is a great big platform
on which everyone appears."

Where infinite streams of young newbies,
in the steps of forgotten has been
act their socks off seeking perfection
stealing scene after scene
The rest, according to talent, cast in minor roles
support the leading actors,
like paralysed telegraph poles.
Then after the final curtain
distraught in belated hindsight
regret not working hard enough
on a no second chance, first night
mediocre performers, wincing to catcalls and names
exit their lime-lit once only, fifteen minutes of fame.

Circle and stalls filled to overflow
with restless lost souls in measured limbo
each brings a notebook and pencil along
to see and record how and why they went wrong.
The curtain rises, "on this real not pretending"
epic production of
"LIFE WITHOUT ENDING."

Enter stage right handsome young blade
tall, narcissistic, aloof
falls head over heels for a shapely blonde
flowering away in her youth.

Two comparative strangers, Daddies daughter, Mummy's son
drawn together by natural selection, metamorphosed into one
together at last the two of them, coiled in a lover's embrace
settle down to propagate, continue the human race.

Detached from the merry gathering, Best Man's tacky pun
nature in deadly earnest, for the lovers lots of fun,
pre-marital caution set flippantly aside
free's double-backed Devil's fingers
for an unprotected ride.

Early evacuation/premature ejaculation
disentangles fits all sizes, missionary position
Satisfied groans, clashed with unfulfilled screams
bring to a climax Act Two's final scenes.

Act three scene one, many years on
blessed with five children four girls and a son.
It's now just the two of them, kids married and gone
genetically programmed to follow them on.
Earthly task over, husband and spouse
sit waiting for death in their echo-less house.

There in the shadows of a once vibrant home
watch again, their condensed transition
from young love to Darby and Joan
Super 8 colour movies,
bounced off magnolia walls
revitalise faded moments, far beyond recall,

on this oft-travelled fifty-year journey,
from springtime through summer, to fall.
Stories one for each milestone over and over retold.
Falling tears at each anniversary,
trace the progress from paper to gold.

Act Three death scene
His pestle is limp her mortar is dry
the play's almost over, it's time now to die
tears falling free from first nighters rouged eyes
blur the last moments of
real-life demise.

***

A MESSAGE FOR THE DYING (*That's all of us*)

If you've lived your life to God's template,
on the afore-mentioned theme
been a regular Church goer, with a record squeaky clean
God'll let you slip away painless, before catching 'owt
obscene.
Large incremental advances
will up your status, to "special mates"
so put an extra fiver, on the Sides-men's copper plates.

***

A MESSAGE FOR THE DEAD

Rumours abound of a new idea, the Holy Ghost is trending
there's up for grabs a million-pound prize
for those clever enough… to invent or devise
"LIFE WITH A HAPPY ENDING"

16

A friend of mine Tom Baines who is now sadly deceased was required to move down south where his job was newly located We continued to exchange Christmas Cards and more recently emails, of which the one below is a sample of what men in certain age groups write about. He is a right-of-centre Agnostic, and me a diehard atheist indulged in many light-hearted verbal rants on the subject. The following letter is a typical theory of mine in reply to one of his examples, regarding the probable scheme of things.

Hi Tom,

Found your thoughts on royalty and religion most interesting, and I wholeheartedly agree with you on every point made. Royalty in its present form can be compared to a long-standing crime syndicate gone legit' whose basic philosophy during its early beginnings was: Give me what you've got, or I'll hit you over the head!

Religion is a fairytale dream of the masses born of the oppressed human condition, that interwoven with life's already established natural hazards proves to me, God and Heaven are invented myths perpetuated throughout time by the illogical superstition that "There has got to be something better than this."

Happiness brought about by modern inventiveness is killing religion while at the same time upsetting our Earth's temperate balance. Redundant places of worship are transformed into residences and supermarkets. Religion is trying to modernise by the acceptance of present-day practices that would have not long ago, meant death to the perpetrators. There are so many contradictions that it's almost impossible to arrive at any conclusion but one. That the only true fundamentalists have absolutely no connection with humanity. They are the creatures who since the biological period began have stuck rigidly to the original basic principles necessary for their survival.

Don't know about you Tom but I'm a great admirer of Richard Dawkins, he has satisfied my curiosity about things spiritual, and during the process re-enforced my atheist status.

The universe, in my opinion, is more chance than planned, there are countless more millions who died than survived on this hostile flying sod. The whole of nature's delicate balance is a mere fluke of kindly circumstance constantly in flux, fine if left to what we call nature, but threatened with premature "life extinction" at the hands of mankind's clumsy exploitive husbandry. Progress is not infinite, breaking out from fundamentalism in our case, is quickening the pace to extinction.

Life comes and goes on Earth, but the basic principle of our universe's eventuality remains unaffected.

Tom. Doves lay more eggs than Hawks to compensate for losses at the hands (talons) of their fellow fundamentalists.

Keep it under your hat Tom, I think I've stumbled across the meaning of life. "Hurtling through space from one big bang to the next!"

Life in all its diversity "from microbes to men" who have evolved over time surviving successfully by eating each other on the now rotting bits of debris, racing from the last disaster towards the next is just one tiny part of an infinite regeneration process.

Not unlike Brexit, racing thousands of miles per hour to an uncertain destination. From whatever our tiny planet used to be attached.

Happy New Year, Tom.

WHAT'S IT ALL ABOUT?

In days of old, at the dawn of time
when life was microbes in primal slime
Mother Nature in contemplation
declared the start of repeat creation.
Varieties of life will grow and mate
in a unique way to perpetuate
forms of life with various span
plus one special item, "intelligent man"
where worldly creatures, whatever stations,
will in death… enrich the Earth,
for future generations.

But Man with his growing self-esteem
couldn't bear to think, one's final sleep
would be one of decay on a compost heap
persuaded his fellows, to believe there was a place
a mythical Heaven somewhere in space.
Where spirits float for evermore
in states of moral grace.

Leftover, redundant, the mortal coil,
is then dug deep into the waiting soil
with relevant prayers the kin to assure.
A bit over the top… for spreading manure.

So beware when Preachers promise
"eternal life, this better place"
sounds profound, but it's a hole in the ground
without any moral grace.
A tiny stinking empty space
twixt coffin lid and rotting face
absorbed in the earth, destined to bring
re-creation in future springs.

Mandatory death, with reluctant cooperation
is the final act of each generation
performed by everyone, on time
reverted back to 'primal slime'.
From preloved placentas, plugged deep into the soil
grows food for life's infinite toil.

What better way to contribute a lasting legacy of life
enriching and confirming another year of bountiful growth
through the remnants of plants and progeny
eternally passed on by the ultimate in physical pleasure.

I don't know whether you've noticed there's not much
optimism in my stuff, well I've more bad news, here's
another smile subdue.

ANOTHER FINE MESS

Election over finished and done,
another five years of Cameron.
Milliband sacked for getting beat
Lib Dems eight, UKIP one seat.
Freed by Nick Clegg's night of woe
expect big changes to his manifesto!

In tow with the Yank's hypocrisy
imposing unwanted democracy
Help finish the work of George Bush and his Pa, and mess
up the rest of North Africa.

But worse than this could come alas
rocketing prices, electric and gas
hospital charges, binge drinking masses
rich pensioners riot on losing bus passes.
Malnourished children, beg for loose change
footsie one hundred all loss with no gains.

Mountain top maiden strips brazenly rude.
God's been forsaken, to worship fast food.
Incense of grass swirling around sacred chippies
chills large assemblies, of fat-bellied hippies.

Separatist Scots spill over the border
northern counties in total disorder.
High on fried Mars Bars, swilled Iron Bru
in unison roared "Independence D'noo."

"Kill all the Sassanachs" while giggling out loud
makes you think on the whole,
they're not a bad crowd.

But if made aware what causes the laughter?
opponents would not be so glad
For the wearing of kilts without knickers,
advancing through feathery grass,
has this side effect of tickling,
the most merciless warriors' ass.*

Meanwhile.
Just down the road to a breakaway group
sucking fisherman's friends to avoid getting croup
Ronald Mac Donald, through booming loudspeakers
grooms young men and girls, into suicide eaters.
Repleting converts from hot sweaty kitchens
Disciples behead… scores of infidel chickens.

Refugee numbers… thousands at most
abandoning homes, flee south to the coast.
Weeping children, terrified folks,
sail perilous oceans, in leaking boats.
Risking lives travelling far
for job and security in Zanzibar.
And if they survive, float anywhere near
get a hostile reception,
as their counterparts here.

This alternative prospect is outrageously mad
and there's no chance we'll have
a future before us being so bad.
Logically thinking, it's not hard to guess
how we got into, "another fine mess."

Present-day life has been flimsily built
with ten parts of greed, to one of part guilt,
on foundations of patched-up anomaly,
too many for me to rhyme.
Wobbling on botched legislation,
thought "Good Ideas" at the time.

Our much-loved seafaring nation
admitted, has much to atone for.
But a couple of positive moments
deducted from the times we complained
spent watching events on the telly.
Would re-affirm again.

No matter who you vote for
before you moan and groan
compared with other regimes
There's no place like home.

*A contributory factor in the rout of William Wallace.

While I've been doing my stint down here on earth there have been astounding advances in technology, men on the moon etc. but all these achievements would not have developed so quickly had they not been precipitated by the

advent of war as best ways of killing people, then in between
wars modified to more peaceful pursuits Why is it that
mankind can develop so quickly in this respect. and at the
same time be so backward compassion-wise towards their
fellow creatures.
The question is. Do we need war to progress competitively,
or should we take time off to get to know each other better?

ARMISTICE DAY

Every November we gather to see
a four-generation-old documentary
where everyone featured from that time and the world
is a black-and-white ghost in the pictures unfurled.
Grainy spectres returned yet again
re-fighting, re-dying, re-writhing in pain,
for a lasting peace, that with hindsight's in vain.
Examples of wills and letters are shown
of eloquent content since vanished unknown,
the copper plate writing testaments fill,
betray an extinct, lost language skill.

Sombre Presenter with a camera crew,
as Parliament Ben chimes eleven
remind silent mourners lest we forget
young lives prematurely in Heaven.
Sounds of the last post fade through trees
heads bowed over lamentations,
falling rain dilutes the tears of assorted generations
Shattered survivors from distant campaigns,
salute chiselled out concrete moss-filled names.

Then wended home in wheelchair canes
mobility cars, cold Zimmer frames.

At night to scramble over tops in dreams,
jump to it lads Sergeant Major screams.
Leaping over stuttering guns
hand-to-hand fighting, bayoneting Huns,
son's and husband's seeping blood,
drown in craters deep in mud.
Maimed and slain, in vain bids to attain.

A Will 'O' the Wisp is unbelievable.
Much bullshitted unachievable.
Ambiguous Greater Good.

Nervous first-year pupil with grave naivety,
reads out loud her essay, on our bellicose history.
Listing recent conflicts, in the air, on land, at sea,
global wars, one and two, Korea, Vietnam,
Kuwait, Iraq, Syria, the murderous fake Islam.

Glancing around at her listening friends
differing complexions.
Why oh why can't adults, like us,
work hard towards good relations.

Please Miss I'm confused, not sure I understood.
Will "WE" as well, have to suffer for.
And what is a… "GREATER GOOD"?

I make no apology for the blunt upsetting scenario in this
piece and the cynicism portrayed, just dismiss it as the
product of an overripe mind, unbalanced after a lifetime of
ill-advised decision-making, during which struggles between
common sense and violent emotion, ended all too often in
victory for the latter.
Anything can be made to sound morally acceptable,
tempered by text comprised of carefully chosen words, from
our over-rich language.

CATTLE ARE SLAUGHTERED IN A HUMANE MANNER
NOT SO HIM WHO CARRIES A BANNER

I've thought and concluded, that since time began
in each generation, there's one wicked man,
unfeeling, no conscience, no sense of regret
no rules of engagement, just takes what he gets,
cunning by nature with multiple flaws,
sows poisoned seed on fallow minds that blossom into wars
hypnotic skilful speech, holding listeners mesmeric,
teases out our darker elements with clever rhetoric,
insanity ensues to approve expansive plans
for killing peaceful people off, in far-flung foreign lands.

And when the war is not progressing, as they think it ought
to be,
it's upgraded to a "Crusade" approved by God, to you and
me.
This holy endorsement of respectability,
guarantees a favourable bias, from here to Galilee.

Sermons from cathedrals, by dignitaries of note,
identify mass genocide, to be the only hope,
for an enduring peace much quicker.
They preach it's been OK'd by us, check with your local vicar.

Destroying evil is a must but not quite sure why yet
we need a few more oil wells, to pay the national debt.
Those heathens are protesting, it's aggression and unjust
we'll make a statement later on, right now though can't be fussed. Addressing the assembled troops, my chest swelled out with pride. Colonel shouts it's in the bag, "God is on our side."

Peace treaty signed, opponents slain,
exhausted warrior returned by train
picks up his trowel, starts over again.
From the craft of murder to brickie reskilled
adjusts from destroying begins to rebuild,
a brighter future, a brave new world
no more fighting ever again,
in a land fit for heroes our women and men.

Into the peace done paying the price,
for many the ultimate sacrifice.
Scars of conflict slowly healed,
been many a year since victory bells pealed.
Memories fade to opaque though unwilling,
of fallen comrades, enlistment shillings
blindings, cripplings, gassings, killings.

Governments come, Governments go,
today's incumbents too young, don't remember
the horrors recalled each year in November.
A century gone since World War I,
the war to end war they reckoned
but being unable, to forgive and forget,
a mere twenty years more saw the second.
International rumblings, inappropriate words,
could easily precipitate a catastrophic third.

And once again we'll take up arms encouraged by massed choirs,
lining up, stood face to face, in leafy abattoirs,
plasterers and plumbers wielding unfamiliar tools
comprise companies of trembling, terrified brain-washed fools.
Driven onto guns in knee-deep cloying mud,
heaps of dead and wounded run rivulets of blood.
Platoon commander writes consoling parents of the dead
agonised screams of the dying, locked tight inside his head
of how their sons died bravely instant, without pain.
A lie to be repeated, again, again, and again.

Munitions barons profit from the cause of every death
returns from shares inflated with expended final breath.
As are the rats that feast upon,
their khaki-clad largesse.

Why has God in all his wisdom, let things get even worse,
can't he alter old philosophy, modernise the verse,
I'd be a Christian Soldier and follow him with zeal

don't hide behind the curtain show everyone your real.
He's been in charge since time began,
is he a frail, done, time-worn man,
lost control of his burgeoning clan.
Folk leave the Church in droves because
they're convinced God's a fable,
a folk law Wizard of Oz.

Win back your spurs be a serious mentor,
encourage the brave conscientious objector,
give back the Earth to the meek and the poor
cheeks to be kissed, not slapped any more,
encourage do-gooding with unpaid labour
make it mandatory to love thy neighbour
In an ideal world with frontiers gone,
hearts and minds would be as one.
Poppy's significance, red beautiful flower
not to remind, of times cruel and dour.

The BBC's mighty media machine can radicalise and lower the morals of those with the highest principles. How? you ask, I'll tell you! By stirring the basic instincts of vulnerable audiences, with cunningly scripted licentious plays on weekday afternoons.

LISTENERS LETTERS

In disgust, I write this letter
to you at radio four
it's the afternoon plays and their context
couldn't sink to levels much lower.

My intense parochial piety
coupled with narrow-minded morality.
Is incensed, dismayed, down-hearted
at the risqué filth imparted
in this rapid downward trend,
I blame it on the new stuff
from the foul-mouthed younger end.

There was a time I could hardly wait
till Wednesday at two came round
listen to the Archers,
then with a cuppa settle down.

Tune in to your latest offering,
wholesome, clean, profound.
Actors, in iconic roles
morals impeccably sound.

They were decent upright with values,
entertaining, leisurely paced,
Now they're racy, salacious, and mostly
concern subjects below the waist.

The gratuitous graphic content
on an otherwise, nice afternoon
embarrassed our visiting Vicar
and my wife bumped her head in a swoon.

Proof of the impact, on her marginal health
you'll glean from the selfie, and note to yourself
from unbiased circumspection.

My dearest lies trembling in the extension
perspiring profusely through pallid complexion.
The vicar departed to visit more houses
that held low down, concealing bulge in his trousers.
Your afternoon ratings have dwindled
by three.
Shame on you, at the BBC.

Later, consulting his Bible, quotes from relevant paging,
calmed his unbridled ranting and raging.
Dissuades him from being ashamed of his gender
glancing down at his resurrected member.
This message from God, through a radio play
reminds him that he, at the end of the day
can still get it up, and with guidance away.

Guilty feelings,
for his Radio Four reprimand,
overwhelmed by born-again vigour
on taking himself in hand.

This poem ventures into the sensitive area of political correctness
regarding unfair favouritism afforded to a certain species.

THE UNBEARABLE

What's so wonderful about Pandas,
why do people stand and stare
At what after all is only,
a black and white veggie bear

A mysterious thing is a Panda
of which knowledge is vague and grey
but we do know because of its diet,
It shits, forty times, every day.

Curious crowds are wide-eyed,
at their cuddliness, "all agog"
not deliberately shy and elusive,
spend most of their time on the bog.

If the world's population were Pandas
living on bamboo grass
and man the endangered species
would it ever come to pass.

I imagine myself loaned to China,
on the first of many trips
Would Pandas turn up in their thousands
to watch ME, eat egg and chips.

A cry on behalf of all animals,
highlighting the disrespect
towards elephants spiders and warthogs
from whales to the smallest insect
this bias in favour of Pandas
is politically incorrect.

Agreeing with the protest
will be creatures of the night
screeching,

the public wouldn't love them so much
if they didn't have patches of white.

This is a story of true love between a man and his motor that
sadly like most long-term relationships with the passage of time,
evolve into twilights of tedium.

LOVE AT FIRST SIGHT

Stood transfixed with staring eyes
in June 2003
admiring her fulsome sexy lines
latest gadgetry.

Glowing iridescent, in deep metallic blue
I was smitten from the start,
what a stylish beauty
be still my beating heart.

Heard her engine running,
an almost silent purr
winking snide of a salesman whispers,
bet you'd like to be in her.

Treat her soft and gentle
as you would a loving wife
then she'll willingly reciprocate,
with the best ride of your life
She's only got three cylinders,
performs like having four

Further salacious comments
leave me lusting even more
responds to the touch immediately
warmed up must 'ave her Coooah!

When it comes to upkeep,
she's a one in a million honey
will take you effortlessly, all the way
on micro amounts of money
Acquisition of a motor like this,
the perfect mechanical Venus
will replace your condition of low self-esteem
with a large in the mind enhanced penis.

We've been together many years
excursions now rare and few
it's only to be expected,
done thousands of miles from the new.

Difficult to prime, enthusiasm fake
exciting hours we used to share
she's grown to fear and dread.
Stalling constantly to put me off.
With an aching cylinder head.

Just thought I'd throw this in.

NATURE'S EXTREMES

The butterfly dances a ballet
over leaf, then blousy floret
a beautiful painted creature
from nature's abundant chest
engaged in a brief but short-lived,
urgent nectar quest.

Plants and insects seamlessly blend
into a sculpture, nature alone could intend.
Links in life's chain perform earthly remits.
But imagine them minus,
the decorous bits.
You left with gross creepy.
Six-legged gits.

IS NO JOB SAFE

Grim-faced Mortician hurries on down
to the coffin makers conference, held in town,
agenda tucked, neath pinstriped arm
contains minutes of the last meeting, plus items of alarm.

Medical breakthroughs prophesy longevity
life spans will exceed, two hundred and seventy
eyeballs, kidneys, hips, replacement knees
Cryonically kept in the deepest freeze
pale complexion? feeling livery?
order one now, free next-day delivery
lungs in pairs, implanted hairs, shelves of beating hearts

buy them on the Internet,
put your purchase in the cart
a world without backache, no excuse to shirk
fit as a Butcher's mongrel, no duvet days off work.
A cash-strapped Chancellor pleads for us,
to be pennywise, frugal, and thrifty
with a promised drop in retirement age
down to one hundred and fifty.

Worried delegates ill at ease
shout we can't have 'em living, as long as they please
infirmity banished, no deadly disease.
Chairman estimates through well-practiced frown
the lack of cadavers will be profound
to incinerate, put in the ground,
but we'll meet the challenge, without delay
through drastic change, in a radical way.
Assuring satisfaction.
Persuading doubters to accept....
"death is a must-have attraction."

Secretary details what the committee has planned
"A break to take,
a still alive wake, at the
Euthanasia grand"
"Escape a future that's all but immortal
Join the queue at our mock pearly portal
arrive in style, wear best suits and frocks
remember the good times, as well as the knocks
enjoy vintage wines, slurp Scotch on the rocks
sat up in your velvet-lined, brass-handled box."

Fed up having seen it, got the tee shirt, and all,
they'll be tempted in their thousands,
by our advert on the wall,
explaining how to snuff it,
fifty ways to end it all.

A once-in-a-lifetime offer
from infinity be freed
we take care of ALL your problems,
satisfaction guaranteed
sign up now, don't hesitate,
celebrate, drink wine
get help to throw the towel in,
avoid long-term decline.

A patriotic gesture on reaching ninety-nine
is to think of Good Queen Bess's health
at this poignant time,
and save her from the irksome chore
She's never found much fun
of sending you a birthday card,
now you'll never reach the ton.

SHATTERED ASPIRATIONS
BY THE UNKNOWN (IT'S NOT ME!) EX-POET

Browsed this site the other day
Write Out Loud its name,
publish your poems here, it said
to international acclaim.
Read a few on the net that day,

some were brilliant, some nowt to say
Some were happy, others sad
some were crappy, unbelievably bad.
Some had rhyme, some without
didn't understand what most, were about.

So I uploaded work to my account
of superior quality in a huge amount
limerick, poem, monologue.
All condensed in a marathon blog,
the whole of my lifetime catalogue.

Wearily stashed computer away
to await reviews, cum Saturday
snuggled under duvet,
for much-needed relaxation
dreaming of tomorrow, unbridled adulation.

DREAM SEQUENCE

Admirers in legions from Dumfries to Kent
generous with helpings of flattering testament,
describe my output among themselves
while queuing to empty, Waterstones shelves
minstrels sing, lyres a strumming,
compare me with, the second coming.

Broadsheet headlines loudly scream.
"Newfound Wonder Bard"
Ann Duffy says, "to top his stuff
I'll find it very hard"

column after column shouts,
"I'm so proud to be a Brit"
"loads of odes suit every mode
packed with sparkling wit."

"Poems for the working man
couldn't be outclassed"
"his natural sensitivity
not to be surpassed"
"failed to get my message in
the world wide web had crashed."
Critics on the Culture Show
mouth kudos unabashed.

"He's SO here, he's SO now"
how on earth he does it,
I simply don't know how!
…Julian waxing lyrical,
to a speechless Winston Plowe.

Cynthia Buell Thomas gushes,
"where has this man been"
why so late to come upon, the literary scene
this bright new star in Write Out Loud
"master of the rhyme"
never thought I'd ever see,
a talent as good as mine.

Julian and Winston, grudgingly agree
that verse for verse compared with me
their work is not as nice,

samey, predictable, forgettable
the genre of three blind mice.

they rue the day getting stuck in a rut
not taking their interests wider
slow to found a progressive school
"like" …Incy Wincy Spider
forced to admit alongside my work
theirs is vacuous, boring, banal,
Winston contemplates ending it all
in his Hebden Bridge stretch of canal.

Duffy, Gough, Armitage,
in mittens, finished, redundant,
seek winter warmth, burning unsold books,
thanking God,
stocks are vast and abundant.

BACK TO REALITY

Saturday night get booted up impatient too,
"bring it on"
anticipate lavish comments, for savouring one by one
eager to glean from ream after ream
what future beckons me
but instead of a toast, from an awe-stricken host.
Get constructive abuse, for incorrect use,
of a fucking apostrophe.

I read this in the Lancet recently it was an article
highlighting the extra costs involved
when someone dies as a result of being super obese.
There are though, ways whereby some of this can be
recouped with a little lateral thinking
this is to take advantage of the novelty aspect that someone
deceased and grotesquely fat presents to a curious public.

CARING FOR LARGE PEOPLE NEEDS A HARD REGIME

Caring for the corpulent I find
the need for a program, of cruel to be kind
remind them constantly while you're there,
why they're so huge, wedged in a chair
grossly fat, a chin full of hair
an out-of-time attraction
for a nineteenth-century fair.

Fast food. slow food, food to take out
contribute enormously to dropsy and gout
MacDonald's, KFC, hot curry paste
all create that overhanging, eighty-six-inch waist
Cigarettes, alcohol, phlegm-blocked chest
drooling down that freshly laundered
outsize hospital vest
a bed blocking, chewing machine,
in the cash-starved NHS
all wrapped up in a big top-sized, M&S nightdress
Nurses brush potato crisps and crumbs from folds and
creases

then finish off with fungus cream
to soften dried-up faeces.

Sister says you eat too much, chocolate sweets and nougat
glucose levels indicate, your body's two-thirds sugar
blood pressure dangerous, and to me the obvious cause is
an abnormal greedy appetite to equal any horses
gobbling down big dinners, cream teas, and five-pound brunches
large enough to choke a pair,
of working, Suffolk Punches
greediness and indolence made you, this big fat blob
the only moving part YOU have
is that ever open gob.

As a last resort on doctor's advice
It was decided to fit a gastric device
with disastrous results one evening
it snapped when devouring a custard pie
and the tea tray flew up to the ceiling.

It's not just your welfare I hold dear
I've got this nagging inner fear
of costs incurred and need to be paid
to our local authority fire brigade
on certified demise
for lifting your carcass off the bed
by hoist and forklift truck
and making the window twice as wide
to stop it from getting stuck.

It always attracts a morbid crowd
when news of this nature gets around
so we'll only have family flowers
and charge the rest a pound.
To see the flying fat lady
flutter to the ground.

Rush what's left down the cryonics lab
preserved in a fridge on a marble slab
to await research in avoiding flab
before festering and putrid
thawed out again in a hundred years
when there's a cure, for fat… and stupid.

I live in a place like this, it's a sort of scrap yard for old peeps.

A brief Chronicle of Life in Sheltered Accommodation.

Early risers wake and stir
unsure of the day, the time, what year
birdsong greeting a fresh new dawning
accompanies sounds of retching and yawning
make a brew and return to bed
Wardens check for the quick and the dead
this daily ritual, and early repast
for some old soul might be their last.

Cliques in the lounge, members thin, and stout
suffering asthma diabetes and gout
tea and toast brought out of the kitchen

effects a brief stay to the babble of bitching
tea cups emptied, pastries consumed
one or two Zimmer framed back to their rooms
those remaining relaxed and replete
continue to gossip from the favourite seat
Have you heard about her, in number three
daughter's researching the family tree
they'll find it easy says my old man
'cause her mum's been around since records began
and don't say I told you, but between me and thee I swear
those before her dropped out of a tree,
and that husband of hers if you see him outdoors
he's designed to perambulate about on all fours.

Have you seen old Bert? Confined to his room
has regressed to eating food with a spoon
according to Betty, he's well and happy
done the full circle back in a nappy.

He was half asleep and sat in a chair,
when asked who's Dave Cameron returned a blank stare
The doctor assumed an authoritative air
and in layman's terms addressed everyone there
when a head gives up thinking, there's no cure for that!
but be happy to know, it can still wear a hat
this news wiped the smiles off the family's faces
the joke's proved prophetic, him in one of those places.

He's gone away now, a week since he went
and on clearing his flat they're anxiously bent
the quicker it's done, the less time on it spent

they'll not have to pay an extra month's rent.
Beloved armchair, chucked out, redundant
clears the way, for the next incumbent
cancelled papers, redirected mail
treasured possessions, on tabletop sale
day by day as mementoes diminish
memories fade, flicker, then finish.

Our Sheltered Scheme plays a game in a league
demanding sharp mental endeavour it's difficult to pick a
team, because at it, we're equally clever
In competition, we swept the board, with a new world record
setting
now we're Rochdale Boroughwide Champions.
At synchronised forgetting.

This is my idea of what the onset of dementia is about.
It could be you might think uninformed rubbish, and I've
thought myself. How can a victim of this distressing
condition be depressed if they cannot remember what
they're being miserable about?

THE EDGE OF DESPAIR

I've found a pen, and paper too
but I've forgotten who I'm writing to
Ah! It's coming back, the subject though
an appointment, at the Mental Health Bureau.
Not been out of the house of late
with crippling arthritis, got enough on my plate.

Think I've got the date, and day alright
not sure if it's, morning, noon or night.

Feel peckish,
but the wife's not here to bake
not here to brew a pot of tea,
not here with homemade cake
not here to say I'm handsome,
how many years it's been,
since our wedding at Saint Whatsitsname
faded photos on the green.
Life's ups and downs, the kids we had,
sticking together through good and bad,
have they been, my girl and lad,
what am I doing, with this pen and pad?

Wake in the morning skies are grey,
another bit of aching since yesterday
my eyes well with tears, in the half-empty bed
when it comes to me suddenly, she's long since dead.
Hell, I'm hurting,… lie quite still,
did I take, that cholesterol pill?

Got a wonderful carer, she's the best,
gets me up in the morning, puts me to rest
prepares a nice breakfast, scrambled eggs,
but the toast isn't crispy, not like my Megs.
More angel than carer tops at her game,
is she previewing, her own future pain?
"A Saint in a pinny"
can't remember her name.

This pen and paper, what's it for,
a reminder to me,
of things I'd forgotten before
did I mean to write a letter damn can't think
and compounding my confusion,
there's a meat pie in the sink.
Undignified, frustrating, the predicament I'm in,
SO weary of this wretched life SO want to pack it in.
Started saving aspirin and planned an end to my despair
did I put them in the cupboard
can't remember where.

The children see me often always to and fro,
but they just don't seem to notice I'm desperately low
can't bring myself to ask them,
help me end it let me go.
Help me escape, this malicious thing
the constant roaring, tinnitus ring.
Help me desert my broken brain,
leaking memories it can't retain.

WOULD DINOSAURS STILL BE AROUND IF THERE HAD BEEN GOOD SEWAGE DISPOSAL DURING THE TRIASSIC PERIOD?

I WONDER

Recycle this, recycle that. renewable this renewable that
wind power, atomic power, all that and then
there's stem cell research for renewable men
all over the world, rubbish sorted, and binned

keen eco warriors' optimism undimmed
blame global warming on cows breaking wind
whatever the theories, whatever the aims
recycling they tell us, will shrink carbon stains.

I have a feeling of de ja vous
this has happened once before
when mighty dinosaurs roamed the earth
gobbling plants for all their worth.
And with lizard numbers soaring, as time passed quickly by
the once abundant forests were in desperate short supply
soon where the green had been was a desolate scene
of barren dusty plains
and today can be found, lying on the ground
Dinosaur mortal remains.

When all the food was gobbled up, enfeebled and horribly thin
failing physiques, bones beginning to peek
through gangrenous maggoty skin
with no food to stimulate weakening hearts
malnutrition and failing parts,
they finally choked on globe-warming farts.

Disproving the theory that they might
have been made extinct by a meteorite.
This latest theory is probably right
an overproduction of dinosaur shite.

But enough of this, get back to these times
with humanity facing an early demise
recycling this, recycling that, renewing this, renewing that
wind power atomic power, stringent new ways
could, postpone the inevitable for a couple of days
then like creatures of old, we are poisoned, en masse
with a mixture of methane and sulphurous gas
Having cleansed herself of Dinosaurs, now beginning on
men
Mother Earth starts the process over again
slow, meticulous, without any fuss,
the cunning old bitch
recycles us.

These days in-depth research is essential before considering
taking up Apiculture, with its thousands of employees.

THE JOYS OF APICULTURE

Two bees flew into TESCO. while out at work one day
both tired agreed to rest a while before they flew away
recovering on a checkout, glimpsed the price of passing
honey
Jesus Christ they chorused that's a lot of money
three pounds odd for half a pound that's a huge amount
we'll have to bring that bastard of a keeper to account.

We work all day for nothing, in flight over health and stream
to return with royal jelly, for that egg-laying, lazy fat Queen
no wonder we don't live long, a few weeks of life then grief,
bet him and his wife share the profits,

the dastardly slave-driving thief.
We must organise a union, and reveal to the world our plight
of exhausting long hours in the daylight
little rest in the brief summer night.

Emancipate our members and then engage in dual-pronged missions
demanding decent scales of pay, improvements in working conditions
equal rates for workers doing nineteen hours a day
sweating in hot sunshine, chilly when skies are grey.

Plus a penny a time for Her Majesty's eggs paid into pension schemes
and sod all for them idle drones whose only task it seems
is arsing about doing nowt all day, between shagging future Queens.

Another serious issue for Health and Safety to note
is the detrimental side effects of the use of passive smoke.
Unless they agree to our conditions and we're paid by way of money
our response will be a work to rule out slowing down the flow of honey.
We'll fly no further than the sight of the Hive keeping well within its environs
restricting labour to ground-hugging plants, daisies and dandelions.

After months of bitter dispute, infighting wrangling, rage
the strike-weary hive and its workers were awarded the
minimum wage.
In theory, it was a great victory but, it didn't improve their
lot.
Instead, the price of honey went up to a million pounds a
pot.
The result, an exclusive market, for them as 'as a big wedge
the only place that stocks it now, is a strong room in
Alderley Edge.

It's good to know this commodity, is still within someone's
reach,
although costing a little over, what the man of the house
earns each week.

For everyone in Britain today, the average home, on modest
pay,
Breakfast time's dull and gloomy, limited to most, to jam on
toast.
Except for the likes of Wayne Rooney.

This next poem is based on fact, the only incorrect part is the
bit about the Vergers bell ringing, because during WW2
church bells were to be rung only in the event of a German
invasion.

FASHIONS CHANGE BUT PEOPLE DON'T

I've had a long life and at eighty-five
thankful still to be alive
I gaze into the flames recalling when
impatient for Santa aged just ten.
Dad carried up presents in stockinged feet
treading loose floorboards made an ominous creak
toys placed carefully onto our bed
Mechano, lead soldiers, books to be read.

Long empty months until Christmas
had climaxed to joyous peaks.
Now the years pass by so quickly.
Seems it's here, every six f… king weeks.

Life has evolved from "not quite too boring"
most of my hours spent sleeping and snoring.
Nightmare-ish with statin-hyped dreams.
I'm back in the army stood to attention
listening to language I'd rather not mention.
Five side football in the school team
Victoria Baths, so cold I could scream.

Wounded soldiers from Broughton House
sat in wheelchairs at the Church dance
by the looks on their faces, given half a chance
would sooner be fighting
somewhere back in France.

During a tango, one turns to his mate
saying what a way to recuperate
I'd sooner be blanching kit in the hut.
Mate snaps,
"shouldn't have shot yourself in the foot."

Me and my friends in the Church Lads Brigade
shiny buckles, badges and braids.
Drums a beating bugles blowing
what a stirring sight we made.

Hungover Verger claps the ancient brass bell
the sonorous, single, repetitive knell
is a prelude to parables on how to avoid
the slippery slope to Hell.

Though times were hard and uncertain
our attendance was loyal and perpetual
comparing our Vicar to modern times
and thinking back to his basest designs
at least he was "heterosexual."

That apart, a kindly man,
with always a friendly greeting
in particular for soldiers' wives,
at Mothers Union meetings.

On hearing accounts of nervous distress
lonely nights, anxious days, tearful yearnings.
He devoted more time to being extra kind

on alternative Tuesdays at half past nine
keeping their home fires burning.

Working days over,
each morning I turn over.
Alarm clock no longer rings
spend waking hours getting weary
passing time doing please myself things.

I'm off to bed but for one last chore,
if I go unexpectedly one night
That's deleting the recent history
on my tablet's most visited site.
This is a tale of how mistaken parents can be when they ply
children with nice things in an effort to frustrate anything
other than happiness creeping into their little lives.

BEING KIND TO YOUNG CHILDREN CAN HAVE LONG-TERM CONSEQUENCES

Drugs! Whatever we think of them legal or not,
those prescribed by Doctors
will cure what you've got
after careful perusal of notes, he will
dispense what he thinks, the lesser evil.

Illegal drugs from a street corner plot
will on the other hand shorten your lot
hooded dealer sells various highs,
to help sniffling junkies
chase dragons through the skies.

We all indulge to some extent
the popping of pills rubbing ointment
a crying child's life made happy and richer
on ever more gobs full of dolly mixture
ALL the time now, he's angry and tired
more and more smarties and wine gums required
out of control, Mums got no money
mugs kittle sister for Easter Bunny
Mother steals for his hourly fix
at her nearest TESCO's pick and mix
In court, she pleads he's only three
please don't take him away from me
I'm the guilty one can't you see
I supplied the addictive candy
I was blind to see the trouble brewing
my good intention has led to his ruin.

Summing up the Magistrate states
it all comes down to the old debate
happiness is not possible
the long term to sustain
with misguided acts of kindness
to a brand-new baby's brain
toffees in moderation
are alright in their place,
but not as a temper distracter
to shut its little face.

Any old Grandma will tell you
that if you really care
one has to apply deep thinking
for a baby's best welfare.

Suppressing moods with sweeties
in a young ones formative years
can mask more sinister reasons
for symptomatic tears.

To all potential parents
if your kids wake up crying at night
spend time giving hugs and kisses.
Not a quick fix, with Turkish Delight.

Poem number ten I suppose is a resume of key events in one's life that with hindsight suggests how we're all slotted depending on ability, to preserve the comfortable status of our betters.

THE WINE IS ALL GONE AND NO DEPOSIT ON THE BOTTLE

Old man gazing at the sky,
Watching the nebulous and cumulus float by,
patches of blue, erratic Swift.
Ageing body vigour spent,
on ideas with motive, most well meant.

All those years, so quickly gone,
friends passed away, one by one,
days come and go each the same,
shame about Fred… erm what's his name,
We were both in the Army Service Corps,
a deterrent they said, to forever stop war,
reluctant conscripts, augmenting volunteers,
helped allay our leader's fears,
bullying corporals, made life abject misery,
hours of drill, regimental history,
scathingly told your Corps "a dead loss"
for winning just one Victoria Cross.

Thinking back of Hitler's cause,
and what if we'd lost that most dreadful of wars,
the world's worst ever, bloody, campaign,
can't help feeling today, would be just the same.
Fighting, killing, avarice, lust,
uncertain periods of boom and bust,
bent politicians feather their nests,
bundles from lobbyists,
clutched to their breasts,
sitting, dozing, passing bills,
on family values, shortage of skills,
peerages, knighthoods, ever in mind,
conservative, labour, they're all of a kind.

Cameron, Clegg, agreeing both,
on more investment, rapid growth,
deep in recession, down on our knees,
can't compete with those crafty Chinese,

with their smoking chimneys, air impure,
downtrodden workers, rich entrepreneurs,
crowded sweatshops, blacked-out sun,
toiling from dawn, till the day is done.

Buttercup meadows! May blossom in flower!
might we ever get back to real horsepower,
magnificent shires harnessed together
iron clad wheels, creaking leather,
cottage industry, clement weather,
subsistence farming, unfiltered sun,
swarming bees constantly hum,
hand churned butter, making hay,
work confined to the light of day.

Damn mechanisation, and all it entailed,
There'd be no global warming,
had the Luddites prevailed.

This armistice day poem is an observation slightly tinged with cynicism of how governments take advantage of the jingoistic nature of their young citizens, turn them into killers for participation in wars disguised, as "good against evil" the true motive being the threat to economic growth or restriction of its spread. Without a thought for the future mental anxiety these young warriors will experience, in attaining a deeper thinking maturity.

It's a poem looking at differing points of view from every level of society, from the aristocrat terrified at the unthinkable consequences of being vanquished, through to

the unwashed have-nots, who at the other extreme, would
not expect much of a change in circumstance,
but on the other hand could possibly benefit, depending on
the reasons for their adversary's campaigns, as demonstrated
in some modern-day conflicts.

ELEVEN. ELEVEN.

"We're here again"
opening wounds, reliving the pain.
Wrinkled ex squaddie proud and tall,
limps past the Cenotaph along Whitehall
involuntary tears run to rest,
darkening colours on the be-ribboned chest,
recalling the noise, the confusion, the fright,
the smell of burnt cordite, the blackness of night.

Chanting Bishop commends the bold,
to the fidgeting crowd, wet and cold
"They shan't grow old as we grow old"
Widowed Mum, head bowed on chest,
only Son lost, sixteen years from her breast,
once gentle features, time-worn, stressed
trembling, sobbing, bereft, alone.
Inconsoled on being told,
unlike us, he won't grow old.

Royal family on the scene
plump red-faced general turns to the Queen
the Hoi Pilloi seem content, to be told
it's great to die young, and not to grow old.

That needless slaughter in the mud
was done for the sake of the greater good.
Can't understand why they never wondered
was it for "quarrelling Royals"
or the Footsie one hundred?

Frail German veteran of ninety years
endures each night, dreams horror-filled
with the terrified face, of the youth he killed
locked in his brain, unable to find
some sort of closure, some peace of mind.
Conscience condemns him to live, without joy,
for taking the life, of that poor widow's boy.

A caring wife prays,
for an end to his plight,
the lack of sleep, the dread of night
comforts her husband,
clasping the hand,
that ended a life, in no man's land.

Pitted bones in poppy fields mould
and I'm sure in spite, of what we're told
would prefer to grow old, as we grow old.
Encased in clay concealed from view
for answering the call.
"Your Country Needs You."

This Jewel, this England, this Sceptred Isle,
steeped in wealth and noble tradition,
rejected many a volunteer,
stunted by malnutrition.

Unlike the healthy fit and bold
with a ten-to-one chance not to grow old.
Dismissed back to homes damp and cold.
For certain death without growing old.

No mournful lamentation no gloried recollection,
these wretches could expect.
Unremembered Establishment victims,
of Brittania's shameful neglect.

This is a little something I put together in a failed effort to encourage a yes vote in the EU referendum. In a divided world with less security, the next and last war will only last the time it takes for a quick cuppa while awaiting the obituary that is the bomb with ALL our names on it.

THE IN-OUT OKY COKY

Get out, get out, fat Boris shouted
hear hear, hear hear, Nigel eagerly spouted,
they're the ones who shout the loudest,
and say of Britain we're the proudest.

The likes of him and mate Farage
dismiss folks' genuine fears
after all, Nige'll still afford
his taste in fancy beers.

Extolling last-century values
worshipping shit-covered statues.
Political has-beens on chipped stone plinths
share prominent space with Peter Pan
and Guam covered prancing Nymphs.

On bended knee, they fervently plea
to someone they're unable to see
watch over, our beloved Queen's
extended family.

As Farage and retro-haired Boris
wind up their let's get out rant
hoping these isles, stay pleasantly green
and be never described as verdant.
Spewing misleading bollocks
praising corrupt old monarchs.

Each week a brand-new hospital!
Nigel lustily screamed
he doesn't say
we could save as much
scrapping Trident submarines
and might as well while at it
archaic Kings and Queens.

He should look into his history book
and since World War I discover
the British have been warring
in some theatre or another
each and every twelve months

of the recent century past.
Must we leave
and chance to lose hopes
for enduring peace at last.

Not one month in those hundred years
went without a fight
the flower of our English youth
cut down in shiny boots
to feed some obscure trading war's
economic roots
If we were forward-thinking and stayed in
all said yes
we'd have twenty odd potential
future adversaries less.
Nevermore to see in an English field
a bloodstained axe by a dented shield.

The modern EU invader
treads his ancestor's undefined grave
as did his ilk before him,
thousands wave upon wave
he's not lately a bloodthirsty savage
looking to rape and ravage.

Instead, he adapts his belligerent crouch
to harvesting
peas and cabbage.

***

It stands to sense that as prosperity builds and spreads
throughout the European Community, the small economic
nomadic groups will eventually drift back to whence they
originated to enjoy the standards of living we in these
islands have un-appreciated for so long.
Leaving us to harvest our own turnips?
Or us (God forbid) digging theirs.

THE BEAUTIFUL GAME

The chief exec. of the premier league
dropped a ball playing verbal uppy.
Saying that dames shouldn't have any claims
on the beautiful game of footy.

Adding. Members of the opposite sex,
physically different, tearful, and tender,
Couldn't professionally like a man!
kick a Beckham match-winning bender
A series of texts, slighting the fair sex
made feminists angry and furious.
Like This national gem, run by men
is genuine, open unspurious.

Our continued intent is to present
a game essentially manly.
Compared to the masculine rough tough approach
women's soccer is namby-pamby
with varying levels of substandard play
the likes of Accrington Stanley.

I must admit, he's right a bit
its effect on speed and mobility.
Immediate change would have to be made
and applied with impartial rigidity.

A foul, "hypothetical" springs to mind
of a female who's generously fulsome
sprinting halfway down the pitch
ball secure in the cleft of her bosom.

Attending ladies football
after hearing the widespread renown
I wasn't impressed with the dribbling,
and hissed at a dissident's frown.
But to compensate for the slowness of pace
was their boobs bouncing up and then down.

Game nearly over minutes to go
ample left winger big-breasted Flo
pounces on a long ball, just inside the box
as referee and linesmen check official clocks.

Setting in motion, a practice ground set piece
wrong footing crouching keeper prior to release,
boots ball into the empty net
past post and goalie's mitt.
Only to be ruled offside,
three-quarters of a tit.

Proving. Tongue In Cheek.
Female conformity by design

was never intentionally made.
Trying to do what blokes do best
no matter how well played.
Spring times here with May the most beautiful month of the year to start this condensed little item of the season everyone looks forward to. Summer.

GARDENERS WHIRL

Mole in hole, Squirrel up pole,
may is out, cast a clout,
dividing cloves, punctured hose,
rambling rose, sensitive nose,
sowing seeds, pulling weeds,
telly on, watch Monty Don,
continuous rain, what a pain,
plant biennials, split perennials,
touch of frost, dahlias lost,
come October, summer over,
unused tools, back in sheds,
snails take over flower beds
less light to see now in the day,
bye Monty, Joe, sweet Carol Klien,
see you all next May.

Did you all have a nice Christmas? This is a descriptive poem of the usual boxing day family gathering, starting off nice enough, but then deteriorating as well lubricated tongues are loosened by excessive tippling.

HO. HO. HO.

The party season comes around
families gather carols sound
Uncles aunties cousin Bill
pilgrimage to Grandma's bearing gifts with goodwill.
Assembled in the parlour comfy warm and snug
dispensing warm affection a kiss with every hug
children gaze in awe at the magic twinkling tree
and wonder what the present is
Santa's brought for me?

Dinner over table cleared guests drowsily replete
Many hands help wash the pots
tired Granny rests her feet,
guests primed up and fidgety
start the marathon drinking bout.
Voices swell in volume,
whiskey chases stout.
Girded loins anticipate
the annual falling out.

Afternoon fades into a cold and frosty night,
waxed-up moon at fullness sends out beams of silver light
sentimental music keeps time to clinking pots
sleeping sibling rivalry awakes to set the plot
Uncle Stanley, hail and hearty
fancies himself life 'n' soul of the party
embarrassed Aunt Myrtle with a glance t'wards nephew Jeff
downs a pint of homebrew without drawing a single breath.

Aunt Maizie sat sitting upset and overwrought,
mildly disappointed at the prezzy she'd been bought
leans into the company with an explanatory word
of the lies about her eldest they might possibly have heard
the slanderous gossip blighting her lad
his petty thieving, him inherently bad.
Those who said it it's them that's bad
got nowt else to talk about, they're well bloody sad.
He's loving, affectionate basically good
poor little buggers, just misunderstood
Aunt Jessie concurs she has a point.
As their twelve-year-old subject
sits rolling a joint.

Posh Aunt Florrie with smart Uncle Pete
come all the way down, from their country retreat
nervously silent while everyone sings
to hits by Sinatra, an album of Bing's.
Listening to my way they sit there and cringe
then Julie belts out all her favourite things
Stan staggers past, on his way to the bog
throws up on a couple out having a snog.
The resultant cartwheel from his slip on the grass
eclipses the moon with his flying fat ass.
Premature night causes chaos on Mars
muddled up Sat Navs lose folk in their cars.

Perturbed at the din, Uncle Tim rushes in,
informing the distraught Myrtle.
He's lying on the ground with his trousers down
on his back, like an upside-down turtle.

In the kitchen meanwhile spraying the bile
sit three Aunties, big Fred, and a cousin
opportunities thin to get a word in
go at it, ten to a dozen
they make cruel jibes at the wart on Jim's nose
bitch about Pete and his second-hand Rolls.
John the tight sod didn't bring any beer
that teenage dress, Flo wore last year
you didn't see it interspersed Ann.
Gave a new meaning to mutton and lamb.

As for her and Big Head out in the sticks
they're a pair of affected play-acting pricks
a bloody big house, five acres of land
paid for from money supplying wet sand
But in spite of the money they throwing it around
their own pew in church, the forested ground.
According to the local consensus, I've found
"they think"
He's full of shit, and She's nowt a pound.

Dust-gathering stylus ploughs a groove
for them to still be mobile and able to move
but all too soon even though they
give in to the demands of this special day.
Summoned Cabbies call each name
returning fares to whence they came.

Closing the door at the end of the hall
Dad responds with a wave to the last goodnight call
Gran sobs it's over unsmiling and grim

looks at the scene then quickly at him
lights extinguished quickly as good cheer
leave unpleasant aromas of smoke and stale beer.

Just like last year "I told you as much,"
nowt like Dicken's "God bless us all" slutch
we've been at it since daylight nonstop until dawn
I could screw Tiny Tim with Gabriel's horn.
As for that lot of ours the drunken strumpets!
I'd give 'em the same
with his angels host trumpets.

While all on earth are sleeping sound
forgotten disc spins round and round
to sum up the party one has to say
in a Noble Art particular way
it almost ended a Boxing day.

Alternative (happy ending) verse.
Closing the door at the end of the hall
Dad responds with a smile to the last goodnight call
Gran sighs "It's over"
God bless us all.

Every year after the party season people use the beginning of this period as an easy-to-remember starting point from which they've pledged to banish an accumulation of dodgy vices, life-threatening or otherwise, out of their everyday existence. But, very few lack the determination to see them through.

This poem contrary to the usual outcome is the story of one middle-aged individual scared into success.

HEDGEHOG HAIKU

Deep sleep extended
by gardeners forking thrust
oop's comfy slumber
oop's awaken nightmare
early death for breakfast
poor sod
bit the dust.

YOU CAN'T PLEASE EVERYONE

On a rubbish-strewn corner of Middleton
armed with secateurs bin bags and broom
Ros and Jan clear litter
for this year's "Borough in Bloom."

Joined by enthused residents
refreshed with biscuits and tea
continue their voluntary clean-up
on behalf of you and me.

Uncovering an old rusting street sign
at the edge of the tidied plot
they thought.
It's a century gone since World War I
and in case we might've forgotten.

Ros. by way of her hobby
paints the sign a coat of white
emphasising a painted red poppy
to locals' and passers' delight.

This tiny colourful symbol
provokes passing minds to remember
the eleventh hour of the eleventh day
when they called a halt to that bloody affray.
One hundred years since.
Come November.

The people on Highways completely aghast
act out of character, very fast
circulating this round-robin copy
"If we can't get at them for breaking by-laws
we'll have them, for being too soppy."

Please!... leave the poppy, to its silent work
jogging present-day minds to remember.
Let it go on and flower
till the hundredth year's past
at the eleventh hour... Of the eleventh day
on that cool Autumn morn next November.

ACCIDENTALLY DISCOVERING ONE TRUE VOCATION

Looking around the conference hall in historic Harrogate
we look a little out of place to other delegates
executives in pinstriped suits. eager to sell their wares

bear down on gullible visitors
with intimidating stares.

The private housing Landlord
really thinks he's it
bet he can't rent out all his stock
without substantial profit.

Which is one of the facts about Rochdale
we're enormously proud to relate
despite a permanent, impecunious, state
"absolutely skint"
tenants think as landlords
they're absolutely mint.

Eclipsing our competitors
left 'em in the dark
made up for the half-hour lost
In that cavernous car park
when the reason for my being here
to me, came crystal clear
it wasn't because of my oratory skills
but to carry all the gear.

Puzzled people homeward bound to Halifax and Leeds
carry information packs
and packets of cornflower seeds?
not really essential for present-day needs
would've enjoyed a lot more success?
with a picture of MD Gareth and his R.B.H. address.

It's too soon to measure impressions made
after delegates talking and browsing
but we hope in the future, to see
a hundred-yard queue, seeking properties to view
around Rochdale Borough Wide Housing... Association?

Money isn't everything as you'll find in this last poem about an extended dysfunctional family living a life of luxury in various parts of the capital.

With huge personal incomes, they are also the recipients of housing benefits gathered from various tax sources including the 20% value-added tax, and squeezed without exemption from the already empty pockets of the homeless and poorest of our society.
Ironically the poor and homeless, together with the rest of the population, are the legal owners of these properties.

I'M JUST WILD ABOUT HARRY (By Queen)

What on earth can we do about Harry,
Sighed Liz to her faithful Consort
try something a little more drastic said Phil
now he's been photographically caught
it isn't just hearsay in the papers she said
that we could easily sort,
grimacing at Harry's arse
front page in the daily sport

One considers his behaviour
as the grandson of mine
completely unacceptable
for the next but two in line
We royals can't afford
this dreadful loss of face
we'll have to find a more permanent way
to put him in his place
In the sixty years of being queen
never thought I'd ever dream
of in-laws, grandkids and nieces,
brazenly showing the family up
flashing their bits and pieces.

Not content with fine clothes silken hose,
diamonds, fast cars, shiny rubies,
the Duchess of Cambridge
got in on the act
exposing her commoner's boobies.

The trouble and worry we've been through
since Charley wed that bitch
the projection of wholesome images
frustrated with hitch after hitch.

Wales's biggest mistake after wedlock
was allowing her out-of-doors
for instruction on livery stables
from office to mucking out floors
the tutor a cavalry major
confused Di with mixed metaphors

on various ways to get mounted,
with and without the horse.

Behind closed doors
in Harrods stores
folk, gossip, pointing the finger
maculate cake and speculate
which dad spawned Jim Titian topped ringer.
Not only is that bad enough
for this cheeky Los Vegas binge-er
it's rough enough and exceedingly tough
struggling through life… Being ginger.

This year holidays abroad have an added risk of being taken
to the hospital not only with sunstroke, but with lead
poisoning as well, with some nuts making it more inclusive
for you with his Kalashnikov.
So I'm thinking of going the opposite way in future.

IT'S GOT TO BE BETTER THAN LAST YEAR

The time has come around again
to pack the bags and fly to Spain
from biting winds, incessant rain,
red runny nose, rheumatic pain.

Disneyland, Egypt, Darem Salar,
Cyprus, Tenerife, Tossa del Mar
a much-needed break, we all agree
to cloudless skies, the warm blue sea,

a tan, and free top-up,
of vitamin D.

Mass invasion by rowdy Brits
Bulgaria Italy, St Moritz
humongous bums, sagging tums
on rubbish-strewn beaches, kids cry and scream
overfilled litter bins, melting ice cream
startled gulls take nervous flight
from sun-starved bodies reflecting the light
off acres of shimmering, cellulite.

I'm back at home now quietly dwelling
on an upset tummy, and below the belt swelling
for not being included in the all-in deal
were unwanted extras, besides drinks and every meal
no use now to gripe and whinge
after fourteen days of reckless binge
'cos an itchy consequence of careless erotica
meant a lengthy course of, antibiotic-a.

So bugger hot countries with gnats and bees
chips with everything, and STDs
I'll try the archipelago, of Outer Hebrides
there'll be no annoying drunks, no overpowering heat,
no stumbling around the dance floor
to the disco's deafening beat
I'll be noshing suet puddings
stuffed with Aberdeen Angus meat.

Devouring fried Mars Bars, marching down the street
to the skirl of traditional bagpipes, Drum Majors stirring beat
folksongs in the local, dancing reels in stocking feet
and the most appealing feature,
of this stay-at-home retreat
is crabs caught in the Hebrides
are the sort, that you can eat.
This is a sad tale highlighting the dilemma most parents are
faced with when their kids revolt against their carefully
planned healthy eating regime.

AN IDIOTS LOGIC

The latest food fad is for us to eat
organically grown veg and local meat
Get it down while at its freshest
Having reached the peak of best-est.

But stop awhile and pause to think
this healthy produce if you haven't forgotten
is nourished by a mixture
of all things rotten,
smelly and impure
horrible germs and squirming worms,
in heaps of steaming manure.

But are the children aware of this
when into their shell-like ears you hiss
eat five large portions of veg a day?
to keep life-threatening, ailments away

But it's not that easy and doesn't end there
won't eat their greens
and Mum's in despair
distraught and distracted with cries and squeals
takes them to MacDonald's, for happy meals.
Beaming, joyful, satisfied sighs,
stuffed full of nuggets, and fattening fries
the ginger-haired clowns won her kid's affection
with burgers chips, teeth-rotting confection.

Mother down-hearted on the homeward ride
full of guilt and punctured pride
wiping tears she cannot hide
reasons, it's the lesser ill
than stay at home,
infanticide.

Have you ever thought like most people do that after all these millions of years there must be only standing room left in Heaven, even though in the early days it was reckoned to be exclusive to the human race?
But think again this world of ours has accommodated the remains of every creature that ever lived quite comfortably since time began, by a process of gradual reduction. So when you're walking down the street gazing at the grass growing between the flags. That grass is living off the broken-down residue of your predecessors, from whatever form and time.

THERE'S NO SUCH THING AS OBLIVION WE'LL ALWAYS BE AROUND IN ONE FORM OR ANOTHER

The passing decades erode away
passion for work, interest in play.
Thirty years since, a loyal hard worker.
Now I'm an indolent, benefit shirker.

Freed from the rigours
of routine work ways
I started a business
to fill empty days
with a brand-new, untried, vocation.
It's the practice of "postponement."

or, advanced procrastination.
For hasty decisions made right away
without thought of what might follow
you must delay, put off today
and think about tomorrow.

Did you know… that there's just one thing
we can't procrastinate?
It's the day you get to pass through
Saint Michael's? Heavenly gates.

Recumbent stretched on my sofa,
pondering how I'll fare
in the un-putoffable next stage
when I give up breathing air.

My first-time incarnation,
as everybody knows
was the shape of a bouncing baby
with cute little fingers and toes.

Got stuck into life's tapestry
began to weave the weft
and eighty-five years later
nearly finished what little bit's left.

Aged ten I'd lost faith in grownups,
made friends with a villain called Ted
wouldn't come in when Mum shouted,
wagged it off school, stayed in bed.

Joined a gang of little terrors,
full of mischief with "up your arse" cred.
They told me there's no Father Christmas.
"It's your dad, that puts toys on the bed."

Been years since that information
put my psyche in a mess
recently, had a last session
for the post-traumatic stress.

Considered now to be normal
having sorted my mental bits
though I still consider most people
unreliable, devious, Gits.

To kick start new beginnings
based on logic, proven sound,
I'll soon have to make the final choice
burn by fire, or decay underground.

Reduced to rich dark compost,
or potash by the fire,
our scattered precious rebirth
mixed with water will inspire
the continuance of prospects
we each in turn admire.

A summary of this poem,
in Aesop's fable form
points out the simple reason
for what and why we're born.

The final incarnation
on this earth
for me and you.
Is manifest as compost
on the shelves at B&Q.

During my early life when it was a five-and-a-half-day working week, the only chance of a lie-in was Sunday morning But Ernie Jones a jolly drinking acquaintance and also Verger at All Saints Church Rhodes ruined my peace, tolling the bell for what seemed an eternity.
The ringing of church bells is a far better persuasive way to become a non-believer than any of Richard Dawkin's logical arguments.

LEISURE TIME LOST

Dawn, the Verger he arises,
combs his hair puts down soap
goes off in search of that dangling rope,
on which his hands will gladly blister,
for the benefit of those
without a clock or transistor.
Grim-faced with each pull
then monotonous dong,
hoping to swell the pious throng
to which the Priest with fire and thunder
berates a congregation,
the choir outnumbered.

Communion,
during which Jesus Christ symbolically munched,
is the ultimate devotion,
before retiring to lunch.

To the devil, I would sell my soul alas
might it still be that clanging
lump of brass
so on my lips
these words I poise
for Christ's sake
stop that… f***ing noise.

Epilogue

Finally stripped of my Christian veneer
lying here in an angry mist
I contemplate life as an atheist
a reluctant Godless infidel
condemned forever
roasting in Hell
together with, I hope
that Verger,
and his bloody rope.

THE END TO A PERFECT WAY

I've tried to please,
put others at ease
went out of my way to be friendly
clean smart warm of heart
innovative, regarded as trendy.
Heard New Year's Day chimes eighty-eight times
seen the reigns of four different Monarchs
heard George the Fifth, do the first Christmas speech
and MP's disingenuous bollocks.

Unaccomplished, pleasant of mind
academically uninclined
a pragmatic, logical thinker
able, efficient, do things without fuss
"So 'IF' life's an exam… I'll get a B plus."

Each night I shower, drink a large glass of wine
don a white dressing gown purchased online
expensive materials, trimmed with black
from the finest tailor bespoken.

Climb into bed, bones protest with a crack
hands crossed on my chest, lying flat on my back
a position I've trained to hold steady.
Then if I'm taken, during the night.
I'll be found laid out… Oven ready.

You've all heard Shakespeare saying "The world is a stage" on which we all briefly appear before moving on. This poem is a whimsical summary of the events surrounding the existence of a random group performing in the repetitive play we call life.
Luckily being married to, and encouraged by his wife Anne, Shakespeare became England's greatest writer Which begs the question.
Would he have been so successful had he been married to a woman like Nora Batty.

William Shakespeare died on 23 April 1616, aged 52.
52/2 = a pair of alphabets.

CRY OF THE OLD REACTIONARY

In Middleton town centre
senior citizens cry and complain
they've gone and dug the centre up, all over again
I hear they say the council is going to at last
make it what it used to be
like in the distant past
a junction of three main roads
where shops were varied and good
leading to Oldham, Rochdale, Monkey Town,
proper name's Heywood.

A neat triangular garden, verdant, vibrant, alive
made to be like it would've been, in 1935
brightly coloured flora, green painted wooden seat
where weary old aged pensioners
rest tired aching feet
admiring ivy-clad toilets, dahlias, and broom
post paying a quarterly power bill
at the electric and gas showroom.
Well-behaved young people, parading up then down
between temperance bar, the Assheton Arms,
dry horse trough, and sleepy old town.

Do we "really" want to reminded of those hard unhappy times
polio diphtheria, smoking chimney's soot and grime
rivers choked with frothy scum,
infectious smelly slime.

A short hard-working, dreary life
between wars in plagued-ridden times.

Laid under the churchyard, having died young
victims of fever, consumptive lung
complaints not covered, by the Saturday Fund
newborn deaths, one in eleven
life expectancy, fifty-seven.
Outlook for old folk, uncertain and bleak,
facing a future, paid ten bobs a week.

Lost in her youthful halcyon days
of rain-free summers, blossom-filled Mays
explaining to grandkids the leisurely pace
walking the monkey run, past Market Place
the hint of a smile lights up Gran's loving face.

Today's generation will marry,
and to wide-eyed children recall
what it was like in old-fashioned times
when summers were best of all.

Why do we resent all things modern,
and with constancy dreamily yearn
for old times gone forever, never to return.
It's peculiar to the aged… reactiveness of mind,
they'd suffer repeats of World War II
to be once more in their prime.

Being born is a most traumatic experience. Pulled and pushed into a cruel world of exploitation. A world where from day one in order to survive, we have to spend each twenty-four-hour period being hardened off and desensitised tackling the innumerable daily challenges thrown up as we stumble through this euphemistically disguised vale of tears. On the difficult to navigate. Yellow brick road to experience.

IN OUR IMAGE

On getting up one morning
God walked to the pearly gate
and enquired of Michael his doorman
how's it going, mate?
I'm absolutely knackered and wish you'd investigate.

Never known it to be this busy before
them coming up here to Heaven
swept off my feet trying to greet,
everyone twenty-four/seven.

The flow is overwhelming,
we need bigger cupboards and shelving.
But I have a suggestion that could quicken commuting
a couple of laptops to speed up computing.

We cannot update, answered God loud but gentle
we must stay as we are, and that's fundamental.
I could stop a few wars to help your cause
and while I'm at it, went on
I'll extend human life, to over a ton

ban dangerous pastimes done for fun
while postponing the annual drought
lingering deaths will increase to six weeks
and sudden ones quickly phased out.

There'll be a deep cut in their pensions I fear
but the good news is, they won't come up here
I know it will work, you can take it from me
leaving plenty of breaks, for a cup of tea.

But the downside effects of my wisdom and power
will result as matters of fact
in that, everyone here in reception will go,
on a zero-hours contract.

Mike, red-faced with anger squared up to God
I've rumbled you, you're a tight-arsed sod
the so-called loving Supreme Divinity
you've enjoyed the good life for all of infinity
with that other bent pair in the holy trinity.
Of my many ideas thousands at most.

sent to you at head office by first class post.
Got this standard reply from the Holy Ghost
and sent to save money by second-hand post.

After deep consideration, we're unanimous at the close
that improvements applied for "too costly."
Signed Cash-starved Holy Ghost.

If you wish to dispute the figures, said God,
in irritated tone
come up to my office immediately
and get Holy on the phone.

List your complaints to his Personal Aide
who will automatically say?
"As you know my boss is invisible.
And no one can see him today."

This next poem is a commentary on when Mother-in-law Mona died some years ago aged ninety-eight. And now being the oldest surviving member of the clan I've only just realised the significance of how this poem, written at the time, regards to my own future destiny.

THE PASSING OF MONA McCLAINE

Conceived in the year before 1908
times fraught with war, uncertainty, depression
children running barefoot, the world in deep recession
jobs were few, unemployment rife
woeful prospects for a brand-new life
born in the reign of Edward the Seventh
through troubled times with George the Fifth
the rise of Hitler, and the Loch Ness myth.

Escaped reality at the Pics
Astaire, Valentino, Garbo, Tom Mix
along a change of subjugation
to George, the stuttering Sixth.

Not paying much attention as the Eulogist rambles on
Raking over times long gone
my mind drifts back to her final year
suffering the indignity, of full-time care.
Watching residents come and go
The odd one rocking to and fro
patiently enduring long hours of monotony
after Doctor Time's merciful lobotomy
left her memory an ephemeral glimmer.
Repeating over and over again
how she hated Sunday dinner.

Daily procession down to the lounge
watching TV repeats, and "Go Compare" ads.
Quiet in chairs on incontinence pads.
I look into her eyes set in that benign face
and softly ask the question, do you really like this place?
her answer is a smile, as a friend is ushered out
through the atmosphere of lavender
piss, and Brussels sprout.

As days turned to weeks long months into years
after much laughter, worry and tears
bearing the burden of ninety-eight years
she exhaled her last breath when the good lord beckoned
freed from serfdom to Lizzie the Second.
Then respectfully carried out
from that damp warm steamy ambience of
piss, and Brussels sprout.

To Blackly cemetery, on a sunny day so fine
the only destination she'd ever been on time
ceremony over, the Humanist paid his fee
we spill onto the car park
to a thirties melody
O, Mona, you shall be free. Oh, Lordy Lordy
O, Mona, you shall be free.

We're gathered here at the Old Boars Head
drinking beer and breaking bread
celebrating the life of our recently dead
Mona, the worldly wise, family head.

Mulling over good times
with friends and contemporaries.
Rekindling sweet and poignant memories.
Of summer walks with Uncle Andrew
trips to Blackpool on the coach.
Might her last years have been happier?
feelings of guilt, and self-reproach.

Calcified bones, kidney stones
fluttering heart, dodgy prostate,
takes forever to urinate.
Find it hard to accept that "I'm"
another victim of Father Time, well and truly ravaged
destined to rest… dressed in my best
boxed up, on a flower-filled carriage.
As Pastor relates to family and mates
round a hole, within cemetery gates.
Of my life and fruitful marriage.

I'll lie erased in a second-hand haze
of lavender, piss and boiled cabbage.

I do not believe there is a God
But I believe in the goodness
Those need image one